PRAISE FOR

Whose Face Is in the Mirror?

"Dianne's story should be an illumination to any prisoner of an abusive relationship. To read her ordeal and then see her emerge into the confident, self-reliant person she is today is truly inspirational."

— Andy Giancamilli,
president and general merchandise manager, U.S. Kmart

"The question is always asked, 'What kind of woman would stay in an abusive relationship?' And the subtext always is, 'There must be something wrong with her.' In Whose Face Is in the Mirror?, *Dianne Schwartz takes the reader inside the mind and soul of a battered woman to understand from the inside out the fear, shame, and certainty of blame that confine her . . . and then follows the brave journey—her own—to find safety, self-love, and spiritual truth."*

— Vera Anderson, author of
A Woman Like You: The Face of Domestic Violence

"In my 20 years of primary care medicine, I have heard the stories of abuse told by women and men, but I've never heard them told with such detail and emotion. Dianne's story put me in the shoes of the battered person."I applaud Dianne for the courage to share her story with others and to illustrate that as helpless as they feel, they do possess the strength to live, and the power to change. My only hope is that more will listen to her message before it's too late."

— Kenneth A. Kenyhercz, M.D.

"Victims of any addiction often feel alone, shamed, or frightened, falsely believing that they must find their own way. The person who is battered is no different. Dianne Schwartz shares her ordeal with her abusive husband, but more important, she confides what she learned through therapy and the steps she took that led to her full recovery. This is a must read *for any victim of domestic violence."*

— Tom Chaplin, Webmaster for Alcoholics Anonymous Website

Whose Face Is in the Mirror is the Hay Foundation Book of the Year. All of the profits generated from this book will benefit my nonprofit organization, **The Hay Foundation,** which diligently works to improve the quality of life for many people, including battered women and individuals with AIDS.

We hope that this extraordinary book will help you claim your own power—and spread that strength and wisdom to those you encounter on your path.

— *Louise L. Hay*

Whose Face Is in the Mirror?

Other Hay House Titles of Related Interest

CONFIDENCE: Finding It and Living It,
by Barbara De Angelis, Ph.D.

EMERGING WOMEN: The Widening Stream,
by Julie Keene and Ione Jenson

EMPOWERING WOMEN: A Woman's Guide to Successful Living,
by Louise L. Hay

HEALING WITH THE ANGELS: How the Angels Can Assist You in Every Area of Your Life,
by Doreen Virtue, Ph.D.

"I'D CHANGE MY LIFE IF I HAD MORE TIME,"
by Doreen Virtue, Ph.D.

THE LOVE AND POWER JOURNAL: A Workbook for the Fine Art of Living,
by Lynn V. Andrews

PRAYER AND THE FIVE STAGES OF HEALING,
by Ron Roth, Ph.D., with Peter Occhiogrosso

RECLAIMING GODDESS SEXUALITY: The Power of the Feminine Way,
by Linda E. Savage, Ph.D.

WOMEN ALONE: Creating a Joyous and Fulfilling Life,
by Julie Keene and Ione Jenson

YOU CAN HEAL YOUR LIFE, by Louise L. Hay

Whose Face Is in the Mirror?

The Story of One Woman's Journey from the Nightmare of Domestic Abuse to True Healing

Dianne Schwartz

Hay House, Inc.
Carlsbad, California • Sydney, Australia

Published and distributed in the United States by:
Hay House, Inc., P.O. Box 5100, Carlsbad, CA 92018-5100
(800) 654-5126 • (800) 650-5115 (fax)

Editorial: Jill Kramer • *Design:* Jenny Richards
Interior photos courtesy of: Dianne Schwartz

Library of Congress Cataloging-in-Publication Data

Schwartz, Dianne.
Whose face is in the mirror? : the story of one woman's journey from the nightmare of domestic abuse to true healing / Dianne Schwartz.
p.cm.
ISBN 1-56170-638-8 (trade paper)
1. Schwartz, Dianne. 2. Abused wives--United States--Biography. I. Title.

HV6626.2.S38 2000
362.82'92'092--dc21
[B] 99-057326

ISBN 1-56170-638-8

03 02 01 00 4 3 2 1
First Printing, March 2000

Printed in the United States of America

To my Heavenly Father and my Angels,
for their divine assistance while writing this book.
To David, who has shown me the meaning of true and unconditional love.

To my children, who continued to love me
in spite of my mistakes and my poor choices in the past.

To my aunt, Lois Hauber, my angel here on Earth.

To all victims of domestic violence.

Contents

Foreword

Dianne Schwartz is one of the most courageous people I know. She had the courage to look deep inside herself and expose the lies and untruths that had been told to her over and over as she was growing up. She was then able to find her true self, which had been buried under all those lies.

Dianne is also courageous in another way. She is willing to go public with her story. In this book, she has pulled no punches and has told her story as it happened, exposing her own fears, confusion, and bad decisions. Hopefully, her willingness to be honest about her experiences will allow others who are undergoing abuse to see that they are not alone and that help is available.

Why would anyone allow herself to be abused? This is a simple question that does not have a simple answer. In Dianne's case, she gives deep insight into her own confusion about who she was and what she thought she deserved, which made her more vulnerable to an abuser.

Someone who has grown up being valued, and thereby knows her own worth, would never stay with someone who abused her. She would walk away the instant any kind of physical violence happened. But someone who doesn't know her own worth would stay—exactly as Dianne did.

Usually the victim knows that what happened is wrong; but then a slow, insidious process begins. First, the victim wonders if the abuser is right—maybe she *did* cause the abuse to occur. Eventually the victim convinces herself that it *was* her fault, and she makes a promise to herself, and sometimes the abuser, not to make the same mistake again. The abuser now has won the right to physically abuse her whenever he wants because the victim has agreed that it's not his responsibility.

Anyone who is being abused must learn and know in her head and heart that being hit is not okay—period. There is no justification. Someone who is being abused should read chapter 22 ("The Mind of a Battered Woman") over and over. Dianne has done a masterful job of describing the victim's destructive thought processes—how it takes place one false belief at a time, building a wall that encloses her in the abusive situation.

The circumstances of each abuse victim's life are different. If a woman was physically or verbally abused as a child, then being subjected to the same kind of abuse as an adult seems normal. Other abuse victims were rescuers in their family of origin and believe they are really going to save this person who batters them. These victims are willing to stay with someone who shows them a little affection—even if they hit them from time to time.

Each abuse victim should look inside and find how this willingness to tolerate such behavior came about. Your life is not a secret to you. The answers are there if you have the courage to look for them. Stop protecting others, and come to your own realizations about what has really happened to you. Then replace the myths of your life with the truth. Once you do so, you will know what to do about the abuse. It may mean you'll have to change your lifestyle, but you'll be gaining the most valuable thing a human being can have—your *self*—whole and with integrity.

As a therapist, I sometimes use a parable to help my clients look at what they're doing. I tell them to imagine that they've just died and are in front of a group of souls who care about them very much, who ask, "What did you do with your life?" They must imagine how they will feel if they have to answer, "I stayed with someone who abused me because I was afraid to leave."

Then I tell them to imagine how they will feel if they could say, "I was in a very abusive situation, but I somehow managed to leave. It was very difficult for a while, but in that struggle, I found my true value as a human being, I know who I am now, and I know that I'm lovable because I love myself."

Dianne has done a great service for anyone in an abusive situation by writing her story. This book is also useful for therapists, in that it provides great insight into what happens in the mind of abuse victims. As you read this book, learn from Dianne's mistakes and her wisdom. Then do what is right for *you*.

— Robert D. Mosby, Ph.D., Gestalt Institute of Phoenix

Preface

I vividly remember the day I sat down and placed my fingers on my computer keyboard, waiting for words to come to my mind that might help a battered person.

For years I had been ignoring a very strong inner voice that repeatedly said, "*Write, Dianne. Do it now—stop holding back, and stop putting it off. You know what you're supposed to do.*" Then, one day while working in my garden, my spirit spoke so loudly that I couldn't push it aside any longer. I threw down my gardening tools, washed my hands, and began an 18-month journey that became a labor of love.

Why would I willingly describe to the whole world in great detail the events of my abusive marriage, and also open myself to possible criticism for refusing to remain quiet about my "shameful secret"? I knew that the reason was that I made a promise to God that if He helped me escape from my abusive husband, I would get well and then help others who were in the same situation.

I also knew I had nothing to be ashamed of. I was the *victim*. I didn't abuse another person—*I* was abused. Through therapy I have learned that ridding oneself of shame is an essential part of healing. Because I have also learned to forgive, I no longer want to seek revenge on my abuser or his family; therefore, I've changed certain names to protect their privacy.

This book is written in three parts. In Part I, I share my trials with my ex-husband to help other victims realize that

I have gone through a similar experience. All my past thoughts, feelings, and false beliefs are right out there so that all of you who are reading this will know that you're not alone.

The second part covers my journey to healing through therapy, detailing the methods I used during the process of self-discovery. With my therapist's help and my own determination, I was finally able to clear away the cobwebs and confusion that were keeping me trapped in abuse, both marital and familial. I believe that these lessons learned in therapy will help you understand and accept yourself without condemnation.

The last section of the book illustrates the fact that healing is a continuing and ongoing process. I've realized that we never stop growing and learning, but can become stronger and more enlightened with time. I share my lessons with you so that you too can find your mission in life, which will lead to true happiness and personal fulfillment.

Listen to your inner spirit as it speaks to you while reading the following pages. It will never lead you astray, but will *always* lovingly guide you on the path you were meant to take. Then use your newfound knowledge to step out and live a happy, productive, and wonderful life—just as I have.

God's blessings to you,

Dianne Schwartz

Acknowledgments

Many thanks to Hay House for giving my story a good home.

Also, to Nancy Christie of Professional Writing Services, who taught me how to be a better writer and made my words more meaningful.

To my agent, Marc McCutcheon, Agency One, for believing in my manuscript; and to Jillanne Kimble, who led me to him.

And to Dr. Robert Mosby of the Gestalt Institute of Phoenix, thank you for saving my life.

911: What is your emergency?

Caller: *Please help me. My husband is beating me!*
Could you send an officer to my home?
My address is 1721 Oak Street.

911: Are there any weapons in the house?

Caller: *No. Please. I'm frightened.*
He gets so violent when he's angry.

911: Try to stay calm.
I'm dispatching an officer to your address.

Caller: *Wait . . . I've changed my mind.*
I don't need help.

911: You don't need help?

Caller: *No. I just overreacted. I always do that.*
I'm hysterical. It's my fault. I'll be okay.

911: You don't want me to send assistance to your home?

Caller: *No, really, I just got carried away.*

911: If you really ***do*** need help, give me a
number between one and five.

Caller: *Three.*

PART I

The Nightmare of Domestic Abuse

CHAPTER 1

The Beginning of the End

I had to be dreaming. This couldn't be happening to me. It seemed like a nightmare. It had started out to be a wonderful, relaxing day. What had gone wrong?

We were at a pool party, trying to stay cool in the summer heat. I sat at the pool's edge with the group of people who had been my husband John's friends—now my friends, too, since our marriage one month before. Dangling our feet in the cool water and discussing plans to go on a houseboat trip seemed to be the only agenda for the day. It was too hot to grill our steaks, so we talked and waited for the sun to go down.

One of the guests at the party, Scott, had the same teasing personality that I do. Each time this group of people gathered, we would verbally spar with each other. Since we both felt like outsiders (we were the "new additions" to this group of old friends), we always stuck together during social outings. He was the only single man in the group, but his girlfriend, Karen, was to arrive later that evening. Now, he playfully splashed me a few times before I left the pool to use the ladies' room upstairs.

After washing my face with water to cool off, I opened the bathroom door to find my husband waiting for me.

"We're going home," he said, looking as though he was trying to control his anger.

I thought something had happened after I left the pool area to come upstairs. "What's wrong?" I asked him. "You look really mad."

"I said we're going home. Get your purse and shut up!"

I walked to the living room, searching for my purse. I could see the rest of the group still sitting by the pool, and nothing seemed to be out of the ordinary. I felt as though we were sneaking out of the party without explaining anything. Had John told them what had happened, whatever it might be?

"Don't you think we should tell Jack and Carla that we're leaving?" I felt it was rude to just walk out, and John always acted as if social graces were very important. It wasn't like him to do this—to just leave a party without even saying good-bye.

John opened the front door and stood there, glaring. Obviously, he had no intention of answering any of my questions. Something told me to just be quiet and walk to our car. If he'd had an argument with one of the guys, or if something had been said to upset him, he probably didn't want to talk about it until after we'd left. But I had never known John to have a disagreement with any of his friends.

We drove several blocks, and still John didn't say one word to me. Maybe he was thinking, or just too angry to speak. I stayed quiet while trying to understand what had happened. We traveled several miles before I questioned him.

"John, what's wrong? What happened at the party that upset you so much? I've never seen you this mad."

I watched him clenching his jaw. The perspiration was

trickling down the side of his tan face. "*You* happened—that's what! You humiliated me in front of my friends!"

I was confused. My mind raced back to the party. Had I done something that I was unaware of? "Me? What did I do?"

"Oh, aren't we innocent? You're drunk, for starters!" He was screaming as he drove.

Drunk? No way. Was I acting drunk? Not to my knowledge. I was perfectly sober. We had only been at the party for one hour, and I hadn't even finished one drink.

"No, John," I protested, "I'm not drunk and you know it. There has to be another reason."

We were in John's fancy sports car, which was small, and he was screaming so loudly that my ears hurt. He began calling me a long list of filthy, degrading names. I hadn't led a sheltered life, but no man had ever said such horrible things to me.

We lived in a large city and happened to be in a part of town that was not familiar to me. Fearing that John might throw me out of the car and make me walk, I remained quiet. As I looked at my hands folded in my lap, I gazed at my brand-new wedding ring. I slipped it off my finger. John saw me.

Instantly, he grabbed the ring out of my hand. "Who do you think you are, taking off that ring? Who wants you for a wife anyway? I should have known better than to marry a whore like you!"

He rolled down his window, preparing to throw the ring onto the busy street. A $7,000 ring! Fearful, I remained quiet.

Changing his mind, he rolled up the window. Throwing the ring into the car ashtray, he screamed, "That ring was too good for you! You don't have enough class to wear it!"

I sensed a familiar feeling. I felt my mind go back in time, as if I had done this with John before, but I attributed it to my fear and shock.

Finally, John grew silent. My heart was pounding so hard that I could hear it in my head. I was confused but also angry and extremely scared. I just wanted to get home and pack a few belongings and escape his rage.

As John pulled the car into the garage, I had my hand on the car door handle, in a hurry to get away from him. When we walked into the house, I headed for the bedroom and began to grab items I would need for a few days, not realizing he had followed me.

Grabbing me by the shoulders, he swung me around to face him. I didn't even recognize him! His eyes were almost glazed, and foam was forming at the corners of his mouth. "What in the hell do you think you're doing?"

"I'm leaving. I'm not staying in this house with a crazy man!" I pulled away and continued to pack.

He roughly grabbed my shoulders again and forced me to look at him. Then he spit in my face! I stood there, with saliva running down my nose, too stunned to speak. I didn't know anyone who had experienced this type of treatment. I felt like an animal getting ready to fight for its life. It was so shocking and degrading, and I felt dehumanized.

"How dare you threaten to leave me after humiliating me in front of my friends. You aren't going anywhere until I tell you to go!"

I felt like a prisoner, but I thought it was important to get to the bottom of his accusation, if for no other reason than to calm him down. "How did I humiliate you, John? Exactly what did I do to cause you to go off on me like this?"

"You were talking to Scott. You chose the only single guy in the group to flirt with."

This was why he called me names and spit in my face? I would have laughed if this had been a normal circumstance. But this wasn't normal. John had lost control—and over a minor, innocent event.

"Oh, get real, John. You know I wasn't flirting. I have no interest in Scott, for God's sake. I think you're feeling insecure for some reason and taking it out on me. Jealousy is *your* problem, not mine."

With that, he flew across the room, shoved me into the bathroom, and slammed me against the wall. Putting his hands around my throat, he started to choke me. I couldn't breathe, and as I struggled to break free, I could feel the veins popping out on my forehead as I fought to get air.

"*You're* my problem, not jealousy! I ought to kill you, but you aren't worth it!"

As he removed his hands and walked away, I slid down the wall and cried, gasping for air and choking. I tried to think of ways to get out of the house.

The front door was not an option. To reach it, I would need to walk within ten feet of John, whom I could hear in the living room, throwing things. The back door led to a small, wall-enclosed patio, but the gate was secured with a combination lock. Besides, if he caught me trying to escape, my next-door neighbors would hear the commotion, and I couldn't bear the humiliation.

John returned to the bedroom carrying my purse—the same purse he had bought me after I admired it one day when we were shopping. He emptied the contents onto the bed, and sorting through the items, he took everything he'd given me, down to a tube of lipstick. I thought of a small boy taking back his toys when the neighborhood children had upset him. He also removed the house and car keys from my key ring.

Then, like a crazed person, running in circles searching for something to destroy, he found my store's checkbook. In a rage, he began tearing and ripping at the checks like a madman. I had never seen a person so out of control, but my greatest fear was what he might do next.

"All you care about is that damn store of yours!" He didn't seem to remember that it was the store that was paying our bills and putting food on the table. Since John had been forced into taking an early retirement from the company that had employed him for 25 years, my store was our only source of income besides his investments.

Crying, I began to beg and plead for him to stop. "John, please! Just let me grab a few things and leave for the night. We can talk when things have cooled down."

This made his rage increase. Nothing I said was getting through to him. Normally, if someone is upset, I find that I can talk them down. But John wasn't hearing my voice.

He ran across the bedroom and grabbed me by my hair. Pulling me to my knees, he started hitting my head with his fists. My ears began to ring, and my head was throbbing with pain. As I struggled to get away, my blouse tore.

"You don't think I'm going to let you leave so you can go be with some other man now, do you? You are such a whore!" He continued to hit me while he ranted. By this time, I had pretty much convinced myself that death was imminent.

When he shoved me to the side, I curled up into a fetal position. But I was foolish to think that this position would protect me. John drew back his foot and kicked me. The pain was so extreme that it knocked the breath out of me. I tried to scream, but only a gasp came out.

"John, please. I think you've really hurt me! Please stop!" I knew something must be injured internally to cause so much pain.

"Who gives a shit, you slut! You deserve to be hurt. You make me sick. Do you think I care if you hurt or not?" He continued kicking me until I went numb.

Then, grabbing me by my hair, John dragged me across the floor. Opening the front door, he threw me onto the front walkway. The shock was as bad as the pain. I saw myself lying on the concrete from an outsider's viewpoint. This wasn't me, lying there in a heap. It was some strange woman who had just been beaten by her husband of one month. The bruised and bloody woman was a victim, something I felt I had never been, and never would be.

Knowing that John was watching me through the peephole, I didn't move, afraid he would come after me. Then where would I go? I couldn't run to one of my new neighbor's homes. I felt too much shame. The only thing I felt thankful for was the fact that our front walkway was protected by an atrium, and I couldn't be seen lying there.

I tried to think clearly, which was nearly impossible, given what I had just experienced. My car keys were among the items in my purse that he had dumped onto the bed. How could I get them and leave?

The summer heat was creating even more discomfort. I could feel perspiration starting to trickle down my abdomen. Suddenly, John opened the door. Grabbing me once again by my hair, he pulled me back into the bedroom and threw me across the bed. He left the room, and I heard him settling himself onto the living room sofa as he turned the TV on to a sports event.

I slowly reached across the bed to get the important items I would need, such as my driver's license—if I happened to die, I wanted someone to at least know who I was. I slipped my car and store keys into the pocket of my shorts, and then took the cordless phone to the corner of the bedroom farthest from the living room. I called my best friend, Roberta, but she wasn't home. Then I remembered: She had gone away for the weekend. Now what?

I knew I should call the police, but the thought of cars pulling into our driveway with lights flashing horrified me. How embarrassing! We lived in a nice neighborhood where things like domestic violence didn't take place.

Instead of humiliating myself, I called another friend whom I had previously worked with. Debbie was much more logical than I was. Always thinking things through before doing anything, she hadn't been able to understand why I would marry John after only dating him for four months.

When Debbie answered the phone, I whispered, "I need to come over. I can't talk right now. Can you help me?"

In her sweet Southern accent, she answered, "Well, sure, honey. I have to work tonight, so I'll just leave the key with my neighbor. I'll tell her to expect you. You sound so upset. Why are you whispering?"

I heard John moving in the living room. "I'll tell you later. Thanks, Debbie."

He flew at me so fast that I didn't have time to click off the phone. Knocking me to the floor, he shoved my face into the carpet. I couldn't breathe, and it felt as though my nose was going to break from the pressure. I heard the sound of cracking cartilage.

"Calling some man, are you?" I could feel John's breath on the back of my neck. "You can't wait to leave and be with him, can you?"

Seeing my wallet lying on the bed, he jumped up and began looking through it for phone numbers or business cards. "It's that man I saw you talking to at the store last week, isn't it?"

I couldn't reason with a man who appeared to be insane. It would have been a waste of time to deny his accusation. I stood by helplessly as he tore my wallet apart.

"Listen, John, I think we need to cool down." I couldn't use the word *you* for fear of making him even angrier. My nose was bleeding and dripping onto my torn blouse. I could taste salt and blood. I didn't want him to know where

I intended to go, so I lied. "I'm going to Roberta's house for the night. It will be better that way so we can think more clearly."

If he went to Roberta's house, she wouldn't be there and would not be in any danger.

"I don't want to see any man. I just want to leave until everything has calmed down." I started inching my way to the front door.

John grabbed me and threw me to the floor once more, as he started kicking me repeatedly. The phone was ringing, or was it just my ears from being hit so hard? In the background, I heard the answering machine pick up. "Hi! This is John and Di's. We aren't able to come to the phone right now, so leave a message at the beep. Thanks."

I remembered when we recorded the message, laughing because we had goofed it up so many times.

It was Scott—the man John had accused me of flirting with. I could hear his happy voice on the answering machine. "Hey, you two, where did you go? We have burgers on the grill. I just dropped one on the ground! That will be yours, John. Come back over and enjoy this party!"

If Scott only knew what was taking place on the opposite end of the phone line! I prayed that his voice wouldn't cause John to become even more violent. What if he thought Scott was calling just to get me to come back over there?

I no longer felt John's blows and kicks—God's merciful way of not giving me more than I could bear. Suddenly, John stopped and walked back to the living room. I heard him changing the channels on the TV like nothing unusual had happened! It was an ordinary day at our household. I didn't know how I was going to do it, but I was going to get out of that house or die trying. I wasn't about to stay for another round of abuse.

Our bodies are wonderful. Even though we are in a

great deal of pain, we are somehow able to pull up a reserve power to flee from a threatening situation. I was running on my reserve tank at that moment.

I peeked around the corner of the bedroom door. John was stretched out on the sofa. Since he was lying down, I figured it would take him longer to get up and give me more time to escape. Making sure my keys were still in my pocket, with trembling legs, I ran for the front door. Throwing the door open, I ran for the garage. There was another door that led into the garage, which I flung open. I hit the electric garage door opener with my fist as I ran past, heading toward my car.

Jumping inside, I hit the lock button immediately. John was already standing at the door of my car, pounding on the window with his fist. At this stage, if John had tried to close the garage door, I would have driven through it. I was too close to safety to stop now.

As I backed my car out of the garage, I saw one of my neighbors working in his front yard. When John saw him, he began to smile as though he was making sure I got out of the driveway safely—the adoring husband.

CHAPTER 2

Searching for the Wrong Answers

As I drove to Debbie's house, confused and dazed, I remembered the recurring dream I had been having about John. In it, I had hired a private detective to check into John's background. Once he had all the information gathered, I met with him. Handing me a red folder, he said, "This is what I've discovered about your husband." I opened the folder. Shocked, I gasped, "Oh, my gosh!"

I would wake up at that point. Because I've never had dreams that were repetitive, it seemed strange, unsettling. Each time I had this nightmare, I felt that given just a few more moments of sleep, I would discover what secrets were disclosed in the folder.

Due to the pain, I had difficulty driving my car. It hurt to sit, and I had to prop myself up on my hip. I had trouble keeping my foot on the accelerator because my legs were shaking and having spasms. I looked at myself in the rear-view mirror. Dried blood was caked around my nostrils. My lower lip was split. My nose was beginning to swell. The makeup I had applied so carefully that morning was streaked and running.

I longed to wake up from this bad dream. I had the oddest feeling. I felt like a stranger in my own town because nothing looked the same to me. The streets I drove on every day seemed different, and I felt as if I was somewhere I did not belong. I saw families driving in their cars. They were normal—I was not. It felt like my mind had stalled, yet I couldn't stop it from racing. I could not be living this horror! It was impossible for me to grasp the reality of what had happened. What in the world had just taken place?

When I arrived at Debbie's apartment, she had already left for work. I knocked on her neighbor's door to get the key. Ashamed of the way I looked, I kept my sunglasses on and my head down.

Once inside my friend's apartment, I finally allowed myself to cry. What was I going to do? I had only been married to John for one month! What would I tell my children? Three of them were grown and on their own, but Derek, my youngest, was only 11 years old.

Two weeks before he had left to spend the summer with his father, I had uprooted him and moved him to John's house, away from his friends. My oldest daughter, Leisa, and her husband, Dennis, had just moved into my condo, so I couldn't move back there.

I didn't want my children or the employees at my store to know what had happened. All of them were so happy that I had gotten married. I was extremely humiliated and ashamed.

I put ice on my lip and nose as I searched Debbie's medicine cabinet for aspirin to try and keep the pain and swelling to a minimum. Thinking that a warm bath might help me feel better, I ran water in the tub, but when I tried to sit, the pain prevented it. I let the water out and took a hot shower instead.

I knew I would be bruised the next day. I could already see the black-and-blue handprints on my upper arms, and my chin and jaw were turning purple. My ribcage was aching and throbbing. I remember a funny thought coming to my mind: *Is it possible to break your crotch?* That was the part of my body that hurt the most.

I searched Debbie's bathroom and bedroom until I found a hand mirror. Putting one foot on the side of the bathtub, I held it below me and checked for damage. I couldn't believe it! No wonder the pain was so horrible. My entire crotch and my whole inner thigh were swollen and black. I could actually see the outline of a shoe print where the leg connects to the hip.

I was shocked that my poor body had endured this much abuse. I had never been bruised this badly, and it scared me. With the pain I felt when John kicked me and the obvious aftermath, I knew I needed to see a doctor.

I was searching for clothes to borrow from Debbie so I could drive myself to the hospital, when I stopped short.

"What will I tell the doctor at the hospital?"

I had too much pride to admit that my husband of one month had done this to me. What accident could cause such terrible bruising, and on this part of my body? I couldn't call my family physician because he and the girls who worked in his office were so happy that I had found this wonderful man and married him. I was going to have to deal with this mess on my own.

I paced back and forth until Debbie came home from work. When she looked at me, she said, "Oh, honey, what has he done to you?"

Not able to sit, I knelt on my knees, put my head in her lap, and cried like a baby. Then we talked for hours.

Until now, I had always felt a little sorry for Debbie. She worked so hard to be a perfect woman that men would want. Every book she read was about dating and how to get a man interested in you. Still, she had very few dates. Now I began to look at her in a different light. She was a lot better off than I was—and a lot wiser, too.

Debbie brought up what she thought was a valid point. "Honey, John never even had a chance to work through his forced retirement from his company. I don't know why you decided to get married out of the blue like you did, but there were issues that should have been dealt with."

Who dealt with issues? You shoved them under a rug, hoping they would simply go away.

She continued, "The two of you should have discussed how he felt about losing his job, even if it was something as simple as sitting by the swimming pool and throwing ice cubes into it and letting out his anger."

This made no sense to me. What good would that have done?

I think Debbie sensed that I wasn't following her train of thought. "What I'm trying to say is this. Perhaps what happened today was John's tension that has been building up from his job loss that he never expressed. Maybe he's been holding this anger in, and it came out in a big explosion, directed toward you."

I certainly needed an explanation at that point and quickly grabbed it, like a drowning victim being thrown a life preserver. Maybe Debbie was right. I knew I hadn't been flirting with Scott. Had John transferred his anger to something totally unrelated? Sadly, I even began to tell myself that maybe I *had* been drunk. Maybe I'd done something to humiliate John without being aware of it because of the alcohol.

Although I didn't want to accept any excuses for John's abuse, something inside me directed me to this path. My heart was saying: "You should probably try to understand

and forgive him. Surely this has never happened before and will never happen again. If you forgive him, you won't have to move again or get a divorce. It would save a lot of embarrassment."

My head was saying something entirely different: "You didn't deserve what John did to you. That man is crazy! How can you ever forget the names he called you and the way he hit and kicked you? Who cares what the reason is for his anger? If you go back to him, you're crazier than he is."

Debbie and I talked through the night. But then she did something that I found very strange. After hearing the details of my ordeal, she asked me, "Do you want me to call John and let him know where you are so he won't worry?"

I just looked at her in disbelief. "First of all," I told her, "I doubt that he is worried. If he is, I think he deserves to feel it." The small part of my brain that was thinking clearly could see that, like me, Debbie was somehow seeking John's approval.

By then, I was emotionally exhausted. Debbie pulled back the covers on her guest bed and told me to try to sleep. I took two more aspirin and tried to relax, but it was a strange place to be. I had only been married a very short time, and here I was, sleeping in my girlfriend's guest bedroom because my new husband had beaten me. It was a very surreal moment. I wanted to be allowed to simply stop breathing and die.

Sleep did not come. Every time I tried to turn over, pain would sear through my body and I would start crying. My mind wouldn't stop racing and questioning. It was to be a long, painful night.

I started wondering what John was doing. Was he sorry? Did he feel remorseful and foolish? Or, was he still lying in front of the television watching a sporting event and not thinking of the violence that had taken place?

The following morning, I borrowed clothing from Debbie. I had to work at my Dairy Queen store, and there was no way to avoid it. I hadn't trained any of my employees on the opening procedures, and John and I had always opened the store together each morning since our marriage.

Using Debbie's makeup, I tried to conceal the contusions around my mouth and jaw. My nose was slightly swollen and bruised and incredibly sore. I still had horrible pain when I tried to sit. If possible, the soreness was twice as painful as it had been the night before. I hadn't eaten and couldn't force myself to swallow anything. I was nauseated, and my head was throbbing. My emotions were just as painful as those emanating from my body.

I wasn't mad at John, and I couldn't figure out why. Why wasn't I livid? Why did I feel deep sadness instead of being angered by the fact that my rights as a human being had been violated? Surely there should be anger, but for some reason, I couldn't bring it out. I was enraged that my life had taken this horrifying turn, but not by the act of violence itself.

Now I understand that, deep down in my heart, I believed that *I* had caused the abuse. I couldn't feel any anger because my feelings of shame were so strong. Every other emotion was in its shadow. What kind of person was I, who could bring out these horrible qualities in John? I was actually very embarrassed by what I had brought about.

I had always had an outgoing personality, although I had spent a great deal of time trying to come across as a quiet, soft-spoken woman. I longed to be like Miss Melanie in *Gone with the Wind*, but seemed to behave more like Scarlett O'Hara.

I enjoyed laughing and teasing. I wasn't a loud person—just expressive, an extrovert. Now, it seemed that this trait had caused me a great deal of harm. Of course John would think I had been flirting with Scott! I needed to change the way I acted. I was an embarrassment to John as well as myself.

My parents had always told me that I was the main problem in our family. I was the troublemaker, the bad seed who had destroyed the family structure. I had not only disrupted their lives, but I was ruining my sister's as well. And now this! I had found a perfectly wonderful man and was tearing his life apart, too.

I arrived at my store and began my morning duties. From the way I felt, so tired and sore, I knew I should have been in bed resting, instead of standing up and moving around, but I had to be there to count the cash and put the money in the registers.

Then I heard the back door open. Since I always kept the back of the store locked, it had to be someone with a key. I turned around to see John standing there. I felt like all the blood had drained from my body. I didn't know whether to scream, hide, or cry.

CHAPTER 3

Ignoring the Obvious

I had no idea what John might be feeling. Was he still angry? Was he sorry? I had married this man who, in reality, was a stranger. I couldn't tell by his facial expression what he might be thinking as he walked toward me.

Out of fear, I began to back up to the front door.

"Oh, God, what have I done?" he wailed as he advanced toward me. "You're afraid of me. I've hurt the only woman I have ever loved, and look at you. You're scared of your own husband."

What I felt at that moment went way beyond fear. I could barely breathe. I was alone with John, and I knew I would never make it to the front or back door. I began to bluff my way out of the situation. "If you come near me, I'll scream. Security guards patrol this area. They'll hear me."

"I wouldn't blame you if you screamed. I deserve to have the police take me away and lock me up. I came by to beg you to forgive me. I sat up all night and tried to figure out why I did these horrible things to you."

I thought of him lying on the sofa, watching a sporting event. Did he actually regret what he had done?

He continued to explain. "Di, you are such a warm, giving person. You don't deserve what I did to you. You just made me so mad that I lost it. I've never done anything like this before, and I can promise you, I will never do it again."

I stood in the middle of my store, staring at him. Once again, the thought crossed my mind that I was responsible for what had happened the night before. I told myself, *See, he has never done this before. You brought this out in him.* My mind was racing, and I didn't know what to think or say.

"I know I don't deserve it, but could you please give me another chance?" The tears were streaming down his face. "I'm *so* sorry. If you give me the opportunity, I'll be the best husband in the world. I'll treat you like a queen, the way you deserve to be treated."

As I look back now, it was not only the humiliation of getting divorced after such a short period of time that made me give in—it was laziness and a lack of concern for myself, along with misplaced blame.

Like an ostrich that buries its head in the sand, it was easier to pretend that nothing had happened. What I thought was the easiest way out had become a lifelong pattern. I didn't realize it at that time, but it took a lot more effort to stay in an abusive marriage than leave it.

John walked up to me and hugged me. "Oh, Di, please forgive me. I wouldn't blame you if you threw me out of here because I deserve it. You look so tired. Why don't you let me work for you today? You can go home and go to bed and rest. It's the least I can do for you."

Bed. It sounded like heaven. I was so tired and sore and emotionally drained. All I wanted to do was sleep and forget. Blessed sleep could also help me slip into denial, postponing my having to make a decision.

"Okay, John, but I'm just going to go home and rest. That doesn't mean that I'm staying with you. I need to get some sleep so I can think clearly." I already knew, in my mind, that I was going to stay. I suppose I just wanted John to worry that I'd leave him.

John smiled and drew a sigh of relief. "Good, honey. That's what I want you to do. Just leave everything in my hands. I want to make this up to you."

My assistant manager, Michelle, came in through the back door. When John told her I wasn't feeling well and was going home, she gave me a strange, sideways look. I hadn't been ill once since owning the store, and I was afraid she'd seen the bruises on my face.

But all she said was, "I hope you feel better. Don't worry about the store. John and I will keep things under control."

Once home, I swallowed one of John's pain pills that he took for an old sports injury, hoping it would send me into oblivion, which I craved. The bed was made, so maybe John hadn't slept all night. I called Debbie and told her I was home and wasn't sure what I was going to do. I just wanted to sleep.

Waiting for the pain pill to work, I lay in bed and looked around the bedroom. Nothing seemed the same. I was in a strange place where I didn't belong. I felt as if I were living someone else's life. What was going to happen to me? What was going to happen to *us?* How could I make this problem go away and pretend that it had never happened?

John came home that evening carrying a large container of Chinese food. If we had known each other better, he would have known I didn't like that type of food.

"Now you stay put and I'll bring dinner in to you. I don't want you getting up." I couldn't have gotten out of bed if I'd wanted to. I was groggy from the pain pill and sore. Bringing the food to me on a tray, John placed it across my lap. I hurt too much to sit. I tried to eat while lying on my side, but I wasn't hungry.

What do you talk about after you've been beaten?

Everything except the obvious. A man who beats his wife, or any woman, for that matter, doesn't want to face the issue, and neither does the victim. If I had honestly addressed the problem, I would have had to make a decision.

Looking back, I can clearly see what I was doing at the time, but as part of my delusion in the beginning stages as a battered woman, I started to play games.

When John sat on the edge of the bed, talking about everything but his abuse, I pulled my leg out from under the sheet. Acting as though I was warm and trying to cool off, I was really trying to get him to notice the horrible bruises on my inner thigh. He hadn't asked if I had been injured or bruised, and I was going to force him to see the results of his violence. I was determined that he was going to feel shame for what he'd done to me.

As I gazed around the room, I would take little glances at him to see if he saw my bruises. He noticed them, but instead of acting as I thought he should, his response was to get an erection from looking at my leg. The bruises were obvious, but he never mentioned them.

I couldn't return to work for three days. My soreness seemed to increase each day rather than get better. I would walk around the house trying to loosen up my stiff body. The most painful thing was to sit on the toilet, so I tried not to drink water or eat so I wouldn't have to relieve myself. A hard lump began to form on my inner thigh that would stay for three months and only go away after seeing a doctor and telling a lie about the injury.

I let the answering machine screen all my phone calls. My mother telephoned after calling the store and being told by John that I was home sick. She wanted to know what was wrong. I told her I had the flu and my body ached. It wasn't a lie. I was in pain. But I couldn't tell her the whole truth. What would she think of me? Only one month of marriage, and I had caused my new husband to beat me!

Sadly, I allowed my life to continue as though nothing had happened. The abusive incident was not brought up. John remained attentive for a few days, but I knew, deep inside my spirit, that he wasn't sorry for what he had done to me. I just pretended he was. However, I did believe it would never happen again. He'd scared himself by becoming so violent and had learned a lesson. Eventually, he even began to complain about running the store without my help, although he was the one who had instigated my absence.

I had pride, but it was misdirected. Instead of focusing on important issues such as self-respect, inner peace, or living a normal, violence-free life, I would focus on what other people might think. A very short marriage, divorced again, being alone, growing old without a man, and being forced to start dating again. Although I felt I was a failure in every aspect of my life, I didn't want others to view me in the same light. I had to hide the woman I had become. In my mind, it was easier to live with violence than admit I'd made yet another mistake.

Due to my own lack of self-worth, the appearance of stability was very important to me. Wasn't that what life was all about? Being able to share your life with another person? I wanted to be able to come home from work, kick off my shoes, pour myself a glass of wine, and discuss the day's events with a man who loved, cherished, and cared for me. What was wrong with wanting that? The only thing missing from my fantasy was the white picket fence!

I didn't want to be like some of my single friends—divorced, dateless, and bitter. I wanted to be able to work through my marriage and be a forgiving woman. Isn't that what the Bible taught—"Forgive one another?"

I wanted to be the submissive wife I had heard about

while growing up in the Pentecostal church. I believed if I could be more submissive, John would have no reason to become so angry and hit me. I could become "Miss Melanie" with God's help. I would start attending church every Sunday, and John wouldn't have to go with me if he didn't want to. I would work on my own spiritual growth.

I found a minister at a local church and made an appointment with him to see if he might be able to help me with my problem. I told him what had taken place and how it made me feel. He shook his head as I explained how John had become so enraged and had beaten me. He agreed with me that I needed to pray more, possibly fast, and become more humble and submissive. He prayed with me and asked God to change my heart and ways. He reminded me that God only allowed divorce if adultery had occurred. I didn't have scriptural grounds for divorce.

I thanked him. He told me what I already knew. The answer was that *I* had to change.

I'm sure if I had listened closely, I would have heard the wings of the moth burning as it flew into the flame.

CHAPTER 4

The First Step Out of the Closet

When I won the title of Mrs. Arizona at the age of 36, it was a wonderful and exhilarating year. A talent and modeling agency signed me, and I was singing professionally and appearing in television commercials. I felt like my life was going to take on a more meaningful dimension. However, by the time my reign had ended one year later, my husband and I were in the process of divorcing because he was in love with another woman. I had taken up an old habit of smoking, my weight had dropped considerably, and I was thrust into a different and unfamiliar lifestyle. I felt as if the rug had been pulled out from under me. It was time for me to start a new life.

My children and I moved to Phoenix from the small town where we lived (while the divorce was in the process of being finalized). I had been a stay-at-home mother with little work history, but I found a job as a waitress. I was terrified of being on my own and having to make my own decisions without a man to help me. The stress I experienced on a daily basis began to affect my physical appearance, giving me a drawn and haggard look, so the commercial and modeling jobs that had brought in extra money were few and far between. My deplorable smoking habit had damaged my voice, making a singing career impossible. I struggled financially and worried how I would make ends meet each month. I was working double shifts just to survive. My children were as confused, angry, and frightened as I was.

No doubt weary of my asking him for financial help, my father proposed a joint business deal that involved him putting up the front money for a small store that I would operate, making monthly payments to him until the loan was free and clear. We both knew we had found the right business the first time we walked into the Dairy Queen.

I worked very long and hard hours. My father's work ethic had been instilled in me, so I took very few days off. It didn't take long for me to get so exhausted that I could barely think clearly. I would sneak home one day a week trying to get some rest and catch up on my paperwork. I instructed my employees that if my father telephoned, they were to tell him I was busy right then, and then call me at home so I could return his call while pretending to be at the store. Although I was making more money than I had in my previous job, I was beginning to wonder what I had gotten myself into.

I was very lonely during the evening hours. After my children were in bed, I would read or watch television after my daily paperwork was finished. I met men, but none of them held my interest because I hadn't fully recovered from my divorce yet, making me bad dating material for an emotionally healthy man. It was during this lonely phase that I got a phone call from a fellow actor who had been on a commercial shoot with me the previous year. I had spent eight hours with my friend Mike and a very handsome man named John while the film crew set up for the next shot. I wasn't looking for a man in my life at that time, but I thought that John was one of the handsomest men I had ever met, while also being charming and very friendly.

Mike said he had run into John at another audition and thought we would make a great couple. We had the same interests, loved outdoor sports, had outgoing personalities, and were both unattached. Could he give my phone number to him? Since I'd already met John, I didn't see any harm in talking to him or possibly going out on a date. It couldn't be any worse than sitting at home every night staring at the walls.

John called, and we had a wonderful conversation. Mike was right—we had a lot in common, and I was pleased when John asked me out on our first date. It was this first dinner date that turned into a four-month whirlwind romance, with John expressing a desire to spend all of his free time with me. He told me I was the woman he'd been waiting for his entire life.

Why did I marry a man I'd only dated for four months? I had dated other men for longer periods of time and didn't feel compelled to get married. Why was John different? Although he started to bring up the subject of marriage just a few weeks after we had begun dating, I could have put him off for years. There was no rush on my part to be married, and although John talked about marriage, he wasn't pushy about it. So why did I agree?

I can answer the above question with one word: *rescuer*. It was *my* issue, not John's. As I look back on my life, I realize that most of the negative situations I have gotten myself into were the result of poor judgment and my own controlling self, trying to make everything okay for other people. If I suffered, which I usually did, it was my fault.

I recall the words of a speaker I once heard who said,

"Every time you feel you have been victimized, honestly analyze the situation, and look at how you may have set yourself up to become a victim."

Low self-esteem begs for the words: "Isn't she wonderful?" What others think of us is our driving force. Unfortunately, it usually drives us into areas that aren't going to be beneficial for us, mentally or physically.

When I met John, he was in his 20th year of working for a large company, while modeling on the side. But what had once seemed to be a secure job turned otherwise due to cutbacks. The company was losing money and started to let employees go with early retirement packages.

Although John and I had discussed what he'd do if he was laid off, he felt sure that his department would be saved. And even though we had discussed getting married in the future, no date had been set because I hadn't officially accepted his proposal, although I was flattered that he had seen my true value and worth as a woman.

But all this changed one evening I'll always remember with deep regret, but which I can now look upon with knowledge and insight.

I had gone home and fixed my children their dinner before meeting John for a date. My daughter, Brandi, who was 18 at the time and ready to go out on her own, was still living with me. Since I worked so many hours, she was like a second mother to her 11-year-old brother, Derek.

John and I had made plans to go out to dinner, and since the restaurant was closer to his home, I drove to his house. When he answered the door, I could immediately see that something was wrong. He asked me to sit down because he needed to talk to me.

"My job was cut today."

I reached over to hug him and tried to be a comfort.

He continued, "I have a choice. I can take another job

within the company, but if I do, I'll lose my retirement money."

"But John, isn't that better than being jobless?"

He was trying to make me understand. "If I take another job and don't like it, I'm stuck until I reach retirement age. I'll be working at a job I detest and will have given up all the money I have coming to me."

It was a large sum of money.

I immediately felt a sense of fear, mixed with resentment. I didn't want to be responsible for a man. I wanted one to take care of *me*. But I also didn't want to be alone anymore. Here was this handsome man, willing to marry me with all of my faults. I thought, *I should consider myself lucky*. I inwardly rebuked myself for not having more compassion for John during this difficult time. I should be supportive, not resentful of his possible unemployment. I had the means to help him out of this dilemma so he wouldn't have to face his fear of being jobless. Of course, like so many times before, I didn't stop to analyze my feelings, but impulsively jumped in without thinking everything through.

I came to the rescue. *I* could make this problem go away. *I* had all the answers. "Well, I think you should take the money and invest it. Let it earn interest and come help me at my store."

"I don't want to work for my girlfriend. I'm used to doing my own thing. I would feel like a leech."

I could understand his reasoning, so I elaborated on my profound idea. "Then let's get married. We're going to anyway, so let's just do it now. We can run the store together. Partners. You don't need that company!" Gosh, I was great! I was once again the savior of another person's problem.

John hugged me. He told me what I already knew—that I was a wonderful woman. God bless us all.

We went downtown that afternoon just as the courthouse

was closing and got our marriage license. The judge married us in his chambers. No flowers, children, or friends. Las Vegas drive-through weddings involved more planning than ours did. Instead of making my children a part of my wedding, they became an afterthought and were informed of it later that evening. Brandi was not thrilled, and Derek tried to accept the news graciously. My two older children, Chad and Leisa, were told the next day, along with my parents.

What was I thinking? And why did I do it?

I did not marry John out of a great, compelling love. Actually, there were little things about him that bothered me, which I ignored. I did not need him financially, emotionally, or physically. I was simply trying to make everything right and everybody happy so I would feel better about myself and my ability to fix everything.

Although I was 41 years old at the time, I seemed to grow more fearful each year instead of stronger. I had a problem telling people no. I would be vague or make excuses instead of telling the truth. I couldn't stand to be disliked. On the few occasions that I *did* stand up for myself, I always felt fearful and ashamed afterward and would back down from my taken stand.

Although abusive men are very controlling individuals, I have found that, in some ways, the battered woman can be even more controlling than the abuser. We try to control the outcome of events. We quell emotions and mask our true nature by smoothing things over instead of letting those involved do it themselves. What we believe to be strength is usually our weakness.

I felt that I knew John fairly well from dating him, but what I had seen was only a superficial facade. He had learned to cover up his abusive traits very well. If I had gotten to know him better, I am sure I would have seen his violent side. I had no one to blame but myself.

Looking back to my single days, I can now see the error many women make when dating. We have a "bogus" list we adhere to. Oddly enough, John passed this "test" with flying colors:

1. Is he a good tipper when he takes you out to dinner?
2. Does he treat the waitress or waiter with respect?
3. Does he appear to like his mother?
4. Is he clean, and does he wear nice clothing?
5. Does he respect you without coming across in a blatantly sexual way?
6. Does he look at other women when he is with you?
7. Is he a gentleman? Does he open doors for you?

Certainly, these are positive qualities, but unless you really get to know a person well, these are not traits, in themselves, that are conducive to a happy marriage. They do not reveal the spirit of a man. Possessing these characteristics does not mean that a man won't be an abuser. After all, I had never seen John lose his temper until we were married.

Also, almost everybody seemed to like John—especially my parents. My mother thought he was very handsome. Of course he was smiling and friendly when he was around her, just like he had been with me in the beginning.

My father liked to fish, so he and my new husband began to make plans for a big fishing trip on John's boat. He even pulled me aside after John and I had been dating for several months and said to me, "You better hurry up and marry him before he finds out what you're really like and dumps you."

John was what you would call "a man's man." He had always been very athletic and had gone to college on a football and basketball scholarship. His life as a college student was devoted to sports. Later in life, he played for a well-known softball team. He was the type of man who could carry on interesting conversations with just about anybody. He had a lot in common with his fellow man and charmed the socks, if not the pants, off women, always laughing and being agreeable.

However, certain conversations between us should have been a red flag for me. For instance, as we were having dinner on a restaurant patio one night, John told me he seemed to have a problem with every woman he had dated: They were all jealous. He said I was different, so sure of myself, not threatened by other women.

If I'd been perfectly honest with him—and myself—I would have admitted that I could be jealous with the best of them! Instead, I sat there and took it as a compliment, glowing in his praise. What I should have been thinking was, *How could every single woman he's dated have the same problem? Surely, he created this jealousy!*

I believe that John was really giving me a warning: "You better not act jealous or you'll be one of my *ex*-girlfriends."

It wasn't very long after my marriage that I realized I had made a mistake. When John began working in the store with me, suddenly nothing my employees or I did was good enough to suit him. Each morning, he bitterly complained how the evening crew had not cleaned up properly. He never said a word to anyone but me. I started every workday listening to him rant and rave.

John also took over the books and paperwork since he felt he could do them better than I did. Since I owned a franchise, however, things had to be done a certain way because of my contract with the corporate office. He couldn't accept that, though, and would argue with me for hours about decisions over which I had no control.

Although I had no confidence in my own abilities, and the store actually scared me at times, it was a very successful business. I noticed when John would ask me questions regarding certain items on the books that I wasn't as stupid as I had always felt myself to be, and he wasn't as intelligent as he tried to act.

It was my lack of belief in myself that caused me to allow another person to step in and take over my business. I'd been to school and received training to learn how to run the store, and I had been doing fine before John came on the scene, but it seemed easier to let him run the show. I stepped aside and gave him the reins.

Work was not our only bone of contention. John started telling me how to do things around the house. He didn't like the way I did the laundry, so he gave me lessons. He felt he was a better cook than I was and would stage competitions where he would prepare a certain food one evening, and I would fix the same item the following week. Of course, he always won. He didn't like the way I cleaned the house, so I spent a lot of time competing or trying to do better.

Since we were working together, we had no time away from each other. I began to go shopping on Saturdays just to get away from him for a few hours, but I would stupidly ask his permission before buying anything, although it was my money.

John had seemed sincerely happy for the first two weeks after we married, while Derek was still living with us, but once Derek left for the summer to be with his father, everything changed.

The verbal abuse started first. The evening I took Derek to the airport, I came home needing a little compassion. I always became a little blue when my son left. John was doing paperwork at the dining room table and I asked him if he wanted a drink.

He kept his head buried in the paperwork. "Sure, that sounds great."

In the beginning, trying to get John's approval, I had learned to make his favorite drink perfectly—a Rob Roy sweet. He'd given me lessons until I got it just right. I made his drink and poured myself a glass of wine.

When I put his drink beside him, I leaned down to hug him and kiss the back of his neck. He continued with his paperwork.

I sat down on the sofa and started feeling sorry for myself because Derek was gone for the summer. I sniffed and wiped away the tears.

"What the hell are you crying for? I can't drop everything for you just because you feel the need to get laid!" He threw his pencil across the table.

I was stunned. "What are you talking about? I was crying over Derek, not you. Just because I kiss you on the neck doesn't mean I want sex. I did it all the time when Derek was here, and I sure wouldn't expect sex with him sitting in the house."

John jumped up from the table and stormed into the living room, pinning me against the sofa. "I am sick of your demands. I don't like you leaving messages on the answering machine telling me that you miss me when you're at the store. I don't like you to be sexual with me. I will tell *you* when I want sex. *You* don't decide when or where!"

I sat staring, with my mouth hanging open. Where was this anger coming from? John had told me that he required a lot of affection, so I was confused. As I look back, I believe he was, too. Sex and affection were the same thing to John.

He began making wild accusations, but none of them

made sense to me. I didn't know how to respond to the things he was accusing me of because I couldn't understand them. It was as though he were talking about something or some other person from his past. What scared me the most was the tone in which he spoke to me. He seemed possessed or psychotic. I didn't know this man, and I wasn't sure I wanted to.

I left the living room to pack—not necessarily because I wanted to leave. I was going to make a point, and I wasn't going to stay here with this crazy person. But John followed me into the bedroom. "What are you doing?"

"I'm leaving. I don't want to be here with a man who believes I've done such horrible things and seems to hate me." I continued throwing items in a bag.

"Oh, God, no, no. You can't leave me. I won't let that happen." He grabbed my wrists and dropped to his knees. He started begging and pleading. "I'm sorry. Please don't leave me. I'll die." He also did something that reminded me of a cross between an insane person and an animal. He would beg, and then he'd spit on my chest. I thought he was having a seizure or going stark, raving mad. I had never been so confused and repulsed in my entire life.

This whole thing was so sick! I hated it. I had never experienced the feelings I was having at that moment. This man made me want to run and hide. Who and what was he, anyway? He hated me one minute, but begged me not to leave the next.

I tried to pull away. "John, you better decide what you want. I have no intention of staying with a man—my husband!—who accuses me of things I haven't done. It was not my plan to lead this kind of life." Of course, my staying with him spoke much more loudly than my words. I pushed his bizarre spitting actions to the back of my mind, unable to deal with them.

John promised that his strange behavior would stop, but he pouted throughout the remainder of the evening as if he had been wronged. I ignored him and read a book. It would be raining in hell before I showed him affection again, I decided.

I learned two things that day. I had married a man with profound mental health issues, and he was scared to death of my leaving him. A very dangerous combination.

I should have noticed the timing, too. Within an hour of Derek leaving the house, John's true self started to surface—he no longer had to fight to keep it hidden.

CHAPTER 5

Looking for a Way Out

John and my father had planned a four-day fishing trip to a lake several hours' drive from home. My father's fishing buddy, Paul, had been brutally murdered a few years before, and since then, he hadn't gone fishing. I felt this would be really good for him, and it would also give John and my father an opportunity to get better acquainted.

But with John gone, I came home every night to an empty house. I usually did the day's paperwork, then I would read or watch television. One evening, feeling a little melancholy, I pulled John's scrapbook from the hall closet. It was a record of his work in commercials and modeling, with pictures from magazines and newspapers.

John was extremely photogenic, and even more handsome in print than in person. With pride, I looked through the album. But while turning the pages, a piece of paper fell from the back of the scrapbook to the floor. I ignored it until I had finished going through all the pictures, then, closing the book, I reached down and picked it up.

It was a certified letter addressed to John, written by an attorney in Canada. He was explaining that he had appeared in court on John's behalf and had paid his fine of $300. The charge for marijuana possession had been dropped. However, he had to pay the fine for cocaine possession.

I felt the blood drain from my face. I could see the court date, but there was no date for the arrest. When had this happened? Was this the life that John had led before he met me, or had he been into drugs and decided to change his ways when he married me?

I was so busy trying to find a date that I almost missed the note at the bottom that the attorney had added in his own handwriting: "John, I understand your reason for keeping this matter private. Good luck on your pending marriage."

There it was. I thought back to John mentioning going skiing in Canada with his friends. It had occurred the week before we had started dating.

What was John doing with cocaine in Canada? I knew his friends liked to party. Had they bought drugs while on the ski trip? And how could I ask John questions without him thinking I had been going through his belongings? What if he admitted doing drugs? What was I going to do—leave? He hadn't been using drugs in my presence, so maybe this was a one-time event.

I put the letter back into the scrapbook, then sat on the sofa and stared at the wall. The thought came to my mind: *Were there other incriminating papers in this house?*

Like a woman obsessed, I began going through desk drawers. I searched every corner of the house and came up empty-handed. Then I went through John's dresser drawers. Nothing but clothing and a jewelry box, plus an empty watch box. No other evidence of drugs.

Was I creating a disaster? Like my mother, was I going to take one issue and build upon it until it became a huge, insurmountable mountain? I didn't sleep well that night. I didn't want to confide my secret to any of my friends, because I didn't want them to think unkindly of John. And when he returned from the fishing trip, relaxed and tan, I never mentioned the letter.

Let sleeping dogs lie, I told myself. What he did before he married me was none of my business. What he did *now* was what counted. If I confronted John, I would be required to make a decision about my marriage. This was something I was not ready to do.

I was even ashamed of myself for going through his personal belongings. I remembered how my parents had never given me any privacy as a child. If a friend wrote me a note during class or a boyfriend sent me a letter, I had to keep it in my school locker or it would be read. My mother always read between the lines and then would accuse me or my friends of things we hadn't done. I hated it. So I made up my mind not to be like my parents—not to pry. I had to trust John, not doubt him.

We continued with our lives, but now John began to pick apart my looks. What he had loved about me before, he now found distasteful.

He criticized my hair until I had all of it cut off. He didn't like the way I dressed, and he insisted on shopping with me to pick out my clothing. He wanted me to grow my nails long and have them painted red. He didn't like the way I applied my makeup.

I spent a great deal of time trying to be the woman he seemed to want, but eventually I grew tired of it. In an act of defiance, I returned to the way I originally looked. It was good enough before John, and it would have to be good enough now. But my independence didn't find favor with him, and he would withhold compliments and affection when I came close to him.

Instead of confronting him, I tried to find justification for his behavior. I always believed that, since I'd owned the store when we met, he might feel useless and out of place.

That could explain why he complained so much about the employees. It was just his way of belonging.

However, his rages were beginning to affect my health. I became so stressed each morning that I felt as if my head might explode. I could almost feel my blood pressure soar. I started getting small blisters on my arms and legs, but the doctor just referred to them as "worrywarts." My eyes felt like I couldn't blink them enough. When I *would* blink, my eyes would not close at the same time—one eye might close, but never both at the same time.

I began pulling at my eyelashes because they felt loose. Soon, my once long, thick eyelashes had spaces between them. I began putting ice packs on my eyes every night to try to make them stop aching.

I was smoking more than a pack of cigarettes a day. In the evening, I would drink wine until I felt able to deal with John and his ways, but then I would wake up with a hangover. My jaw ached because I was clenching and grinding my teeth constantly. My dentist told me I was on my way to getting TMJ, a disorder of the jaw. I suffered from diarrhea daily, and my back would go into painful spasms with the muscles "jumping" and twitching. Obviously, my body was trying to tell me something, but I wasn't listening.

By this time, John was smoking pot daily and openly in front of me. This man who had pretended to be drug free was stoned every night. Despite my feelings about drugs, I welcomed it. When he was high, he grew relaxed. He would laugh and joke, and it made my life much easier. It was the only way I could be around him and not be afraid. I grew to understand how a habit such as drinking could become a crutch to help cope with life. If life was still unbearable, it became an addiction, and I felt I was on my way to becoming an alcoholic.

Then, John wanted me to go on a houseboat trip with

all his friends for one week. I didn't really want to go. It wasn't that I didn't like his friends—most of them were nice, but they lived a different life than I was accustomed to. They did nothing but drink and smoke pot every time they got together. One week of that, trapped on a houseboat in the middle of a lake, was more than I could stand. I begged off.

John was infuriated with me. How could I do this to him? It made him look bad in front of his friends. I told him I wasn't comfortable leaving the store for that amount of time. I told him to go without me, that I didn't care. We argued for two weeks and finally came to an agreement. He would go ahead of me for four days, and I would fly on a commuter plane to the lake and meet him at the marina and spend the three remaining days with him and his friends.

What I dreaded became a reality: three days of drinking and stupidity. I tried to be friendly, but I was more miserable than I had been in ages. When the large tour boats would pass by, one of the men would pull down their shorts and "moon" the tourists. It was humiliating. They weren't teenagers. These were grown men behaving in this way. John's boat was even used for water skiing in the nude.

Every night we played a game of quarters. We would try to flip a quarter into a shot glass, and if we succeeded, we would point to one of the members of the group. That person would have to drink a shot of tequila. If we missed the shot glass, we had to drink a shot ourselves. Stupid game.

John had one friend who didn't like me. I had been friendly with one of his old girlfriends years before, so he might have thought I knew things about him. Each time he would successfully get the quarter in the glass, he would point to me. I guess it was his way of trying to get to me. But what he didn't know was that I have a strange system. If I drink wine or hard liquor, I usually feel the effects after one glass. However, tequila doesn't bother me. I can drink it all night long and never feel anything. I won't get drunk or have a hangover the next morning. So his efforts to make me sick failed. I felt like a fool for being part of the game.

I couldn't wait to get back home. I was lonely and felt out of place. And to make matters worse, John had treated me like a stranger the entire time I was there. I knew I should have listened to my instincts and stayed home. The morning we left to head back home, John and I rode alone in his truck. He told me he knew I had not had a good time, but he gave me credit for trying. Then he started telling me of the group's latest plans. We were all going to go on a trip to Canada and spend a week on a boat. I didn't want to even pretend that I was going.

"No, John," I said firmly. "I'm not going on that trip. You can go, but leave me out."

He immediately grew angry. "Are you telling me that you aren't going to do anything with my friends again?"

I grew hesitant. We had a long drive ahead of us, and I didn't want to spend it fighting. So I tried to come up with an alternative.

"What would be wrong with us forming new friendships? I don't think it's good for our marriage to only associate with the people who knew you before. We never go anywhere or do anything unless it's with this group of people. I want to make new friends together."

But what made sense to me angered him. My fears were realized—we argued the entire trip. When we neared home, I grew nervous. We had to stop at one of his friend's homes to retrieve our camping gear, and I didn't want his friends to know we had been fighting. I backed down and put on my happy face to calm him down and make him believe we would continue going everywhere with his friends. When we arrived at our destination, I laughed and joked and pretended all was well, but he was still angry.

After spending yet another evening dealing with John's anger and hostility, plus facing the truth about spending the remainder of my life with this abusive man as well as every vacation with his friends, I finally decided I'd had enough. This was not the way I wanted the second half of my life to be.

The following morning, I decided to talk with John while he was calm. We were sitting on the patio, drinking coffee.

"John, I need to talk to you about something important." I waited until he gave me his attention before continuing. "We don't seem to get along on any issues. We fight and argue about everything. I'm sure at our age, we had different plans for our life."

He was staring at me with no reaction. I took a deep breath and continued. "Sometimes people just have to admit they've made a mistake and go from there. We haven't been married very long, so maybe we could get an annulment. We could part as friends instead of destroying each other, like we seem to be doing."

There. It was out in the open. John continued to stare at me, but I couldn't tell what he was thinking. Suddenly, he threw his coffee in my face. When I turned my face away, he hit me on the side of my head with his coffee mug. "You try to leave me and I'll kill you."

I had no doubt whatsoever that John meant what he said. He was perfectly capable of bringing about my death. His greatest fear seemed to be me walking out the door, never to return. He would stop at nothing to get even with me for deserting him.

I didn't understand the dynamics of abandonment at that point of my life, but it seemed that this was one of John's emotional buttons. I don't believe that either of us could see that he had abandoned our marriage the first time he hit me.

With those words, I became a prisoner. I took a shower behind a locked bathroom door because of my fear, wondering if he would decide to kill me at that moment, and then we both went to work. Once there, I acted like nothing had happened. As usual, I needed to appear normal, but we avoided each other all day.

It was on that day that I began to think of ways to leave John without creating harm or danger to myself. I thought he might feel dependent on me because of the store. After all, it was his only source of income except for the interest he received each month on his investments. If I could talk him into buying his own business, I would get him out of my store and perhaps take his fear of desertion away. But I had to be careful about my timing because I didn't want to be beaten again.

The right time came along sooner than expected. I had tried many times before to explain to John how his rages at work created stress. One morning upon entering the store, he started into one of his usual sessions about the night crew. I sat down and began to cry.

"I'm sorry," he explained. "I try not to do this every morning, but I can't seem to help myself."

It was the perfect opening. "John, I don't believe you're happy here. That's why you look for things to complain about. Wouldn't you be happier if you bought your own business and could run it the way you wanted to?"

He didn't become angry, so feeling encouraged, I gave him the name of a business broker I knew. I had planted a seed and could only hope and pray it took root.

Within three weeks, John had found a business that would be perfect for him: a sports bar. I felt like I could breathe again. Soon I wouldn't have to spend all my days and nights with him. It would be a step toward freedom, if he didn't kill me first.

CHAPTER 6

The Introduction into His World

I believed my own lies when I thought John might change after buying his own business. I was gullible enough to think that his anger stemmed from not being his own man. I grasped at excuses. I'd only seen the tip of the iceberg. Like a ship in the night with no captain on board, I was headed for a huge disaster.

What creates sexual deviation? I don't know. I only know what angst and pain it caused in my life. There didn't seem to be enough sex on the planet to satisfy John. And it wasn't the kind of sex I was familiar or comfortable with. One kind of perversion seemed to lead to another. What men may laugh about in the locker room regarding their sexual prowess was one thing, but John had a sickness when it came to sexual matters.

When we first married, John seemed to be normal sexually, although he told me he required a lot of affection. In the beginning, it felt good to be wanted. But soon I began to feel I had to perform on demand. And once the abuse was part of our relationship, it was impossible for me to feign desire for a man who beat me. I hated his touch.

Along with his abusive behavior, John began to stray into areas I didn't want anything to do with. He was drinking heavily and was smoking pot every night, so he no longer knew what was going on during intimate moments. He was drunk *and* high, unable to enjoy sex without a buzz. And I detested it. Then he purchased a small bottle of a chemical called a "popper" to inhale right before reaching orgasm. He encouraged me participate in this new thrill, but I refused. This bottle of magic liquid that was supposed to enhance his experience would actually cause John to lose his erection, and he wouldn't even know it. He was in another world.

Along with John's use of alcohol, drugs, and poppers, he took another step into perversion when, during lovemaking, he wanted me to tell him about other sexual experiences I'd had. I didn't want to discuss this with John. I knew this could be unhealthy for a relationship, and I had no desire to tread into dangerous waters. This behavior was *not* a turn-on for me, but he never gave up.

John would also tell me in great detail about what he had done with other women. Hearing about his exploits nauseated me. After all, we were husband and wife, and some things are better left unsaid. He mentioned so many different women that I wondered if there'd been a revolving door in his bedroom.

There didn't seem to be anything stopping John in his quest for more bizarre sex as he concocted new ideas every night. He decided that I should find another woman to go to bed with us. I threw a fit! I wasn't about to share my husband with another woman. To me, making love was a sacred act between a husband and wife, and was not meant to be shared with others.

Every night when I would come home from work, he

would ask me if I had found another woman even though I had told him from the start that I wasn't going to be a participant in his stupid plan. But he ignored me, and each time he asked me if I had found someone, my response was a very sarcastic, "Nope."

John said he wanted us to go to a porno theater, but I refused. If he wanted to watch trash that I felt demeaned women, he could do it on his own. Never one to give up, he started bringing home sleazy newspapers, printed about and for wife-swapping couples and their private parties. He was like a hunter on a mission for prey, and I was tired of his relentless pursuit of new ways to satisfy his sickness.

Perversion is much more than just fulfilling sexual needs and desires. It's another way in which the abuser can degrade his victim, because the beatings aren't giving him the satisfaction and control he needs, and his illness isn't being fed.

John's type of abuse rendered me a sexual object, not a woman or even a human being. His fantasies were the type that would always put me in the position of lowering or exposing myself in compromising, if not humiliating, situations. I was nothing more than someone to use while he watched, or when he required me to watch *him* as he pleasured himself.

I was not viewed as a wife to be cherished and honored, and I wasn't held in high regard or respected in any shape or form. Actually, I was no different from any other woman on the street who could gratify his needs. A prostitute would have performed the same function.

There is a *very* strong dynamic that takes place when the victim refuses to take part in this kind of aberrant behavior. The relationship is immediately thrown into the tension-building phase that is different from the regular show of disapproval during the domestic violence cycle.

Normally in an abusive marriage, the explosion stage takes place after the victim has agonizingly attempted to survive the tension-building phase. She knows that once the abuser has built up his anger and has discharged it by assaulting her—verbally or physically—he will once again calm down as they enter the honeymoon part of the cycle. But when she continually refuses to give in to certain demands, the abuser's anger does not diminish. His hostility will persist until she gives in. He will make the victim's life unbearable until she agrees to go along with his demands.

Unless a person has experienced this trauma, it is inexplicable how absolutely horrifying and nerve-wracking it is to try and live like this. You go back and forth between tension building and explosion, with no reprieve.

I was aware that all I had to do was give in to John's sexual demands and perversions, and he would once again consider me "his girl," but I had reached my limit and set a boundary that I'd never remove—and he hated it. This was an area of my life he couldn't control. However, I was living with horror and revulsion, slowly becoming a stranger to myself because I hadn't been raised with this kind of filth and disgust. Where would all of this end? How had I been pulled into this dark and degrading lifestyle?

As John's resentment toward me increased, so did his physical violence. He was grabbing me by the throat and slamming me into walls and through doors on a regular basis. I always had a bruise somewhere on my body.

His violence even became sexual. He would hold me down on the bed and pinch and punch at my breasts or vagina. Then he would throw me off the bed onto the floor in disgust, while calling me filthy names. When I threatened to leave, he threatened to kill me. I was afraid to start my car in the morning for fear of a bomb going off. John was psychotic, and I wasn't in much better shape.

If I hadn't had my store to run, I would have gone to a shelter. I called a local battered woman's house, but their rules stipulated that, once I arrived, I could not leave for one week. There was no one to run the store for me, so I had to find another way. I didn't want to stay with friends and possibly bring harm to them if John stalked me. I prayed daily for safety until I could flee.

I was also once again suffering from shame and blame, along with John's distorted demands. Like a woman who receives obscene phone calls from the same man on many occasions, I began to feel that there might be something about me that caused John's sexual problems. Had I done or said something that brought out this side of him? He had seemed so normal in the beginning. Maybe I was too strict in my opinions about sex. Perhaps *I* was the one with a problem, as he had told me on more than one occasion.

Society doesn't understand why a woman cannot just pack up and go. But a woman is in the greatest danger when she leaves her abuser. He feels the loss of control over her life and usually gets more violent. He needs to make her step back into the same pattern and behave. According to Bureau of Justice statistics, a separated or divorced woman is 14 times more likely than a married woman to report having been a victim of violence by her spouse or ex-spouse[1] because she now feels safe enough to speak the truth.

Some women who have left an abusive partner have been followed and harassed for months or even years; some have even been killed. Evidence suggests that, in many cases, the man's violence continues to escalate after a separation. In a 1980 report to the Wisconsin Council on Criminal Justice, 30 percent of the assaulted women in that study were separated from their partners when the attack occurred.[2]

Some battered women don't have the money to leave. A lot of them don't work—at their husband's request or demand. I had the money but was simply afraid to escape. I was also in very deep denial while minimizing John's abuse. I had read about so many women who had been battered much worse than I had been.

Once again, attempting to be the rescuer, I tried to understand what made John so angry and abusive. He said he had never hit a woman until he'd met me, so what was happening between us to create this violence?

I thought about his background. John's father became a millionaire overnight because of an invention, and the family moved from a middle-class neighborhood to one where the elite and famous lived. Not long after that, John, who was 12 at that time, came home from school to find his mother crying at the dining room table, holding a letter from his father. He had written to tell her he was divorcing her and marrying a Las Vegas showgirl. He hadn't bothered to talk to her in person.

John only talked to his father a few times after that, and only on the telephone. Soon, he refused to speak to him at all. John's two younger sisters suffered this humiliation and heartache, also. This situation could have formed the basis for John's underlying anger, but it certainly didn't make sense that it made him a woman-hater. But I was never to receive the whole story because John wouldn't speak about it. I had to piece stories together to get the picture.

It seems that there was a man who had previously worked with John's father. I believe he befriended John's mother after her husband left her. Eventually, their friendship turned into romance and they began to live together. In this modern era, living together is common, but it wasn't acceptable 30 or 40 years ago. It was considered cheap and vulgar. Respectable people did not cohabitate. As a result, I believe that a lot a shame was brought upon John and his sisters. I'm sure the neighborhood children taunted them.

To make matters worse, when his mother married this man and he became the stepfather, life changed for John. From what he and his sister told me, this man was very strict and controlling. If John sassed his mother, he was hit in the mouth with a fist that sent him flying across the room. As teenagers, his sisters were degraded in front of their friends by receiving spankings at the bus stop in front of their peers.

John's mother always seemed like a kind, giving woman, and I had always liked her. When I told her I suffered from asthma, she said her second husband also had this ailment. She said he slept with an inhaler in his hand at night, and if she heard him drop the inhaler on the floor in his sleep, she would jump up and crawl on her hands and knees in the dark to find it for him. I believe she did everything her husband desired and did not cross him in any way.

One morning, John told me a very revealing story about his stepfather. Because of his severe asthma and the strain on his body, his stepfather developed a weakened heart. Finally, he landed in the hospital and was not expected to live much longer. The last time John spoke with him, before his death, he told John that he considered him the best ball player he had ever seen. As John told me this, he began to cry.

From what I could gather, these were the only kind words the man had ever spoken to John. I couldn't imagine these being a man's last words to his stepson. No words of love or sorrow—just baseball. What kind of teenage years did John endure?

I didn't think John's stepfather made him a misogynist. After all, John spoke highly of his mother. I think he believed it was a deep sin to speak harshly of her. However, I think he resented his mother—maybe even hated her—for allowing some man to come into their life and treat them so horribly.

Although he professed love for his mother, John never called her or saw her, even though she lived in the same town. As she grew older, John would speak about her inevitable passing and how much he was going to grieve for her, almost as though he were planning how to act rather than dreading her death. Perhaps, since he was not able to admit to hating his mother, he hated other women instead.

John's sister eventually hired a private detective to find their father, since they hadn't heard from him in over 30 years. He was married and living in the Southeast. Once contacted, he immediately flew out to see his children, despite being in very poor health.

It was very uncomfortable meeting him. He never asked John anything about his life, but only spoke of what he had been doing. He returned to his home, but flew out a few weeks later to visit again. By this time, he had to hook up to an IV every night to survive, but John refused to see him during his second trip.

Then, he wrote us a letter professing his love for John, saying how much he missed him, but John refused to answer the letter or allow me to either. He died a month later.

I never met John's youngest sister, whom John described as "troubled." He said she was divorced, did drugs, and if she didn't get her way, she threw terrible temper tantrums. He also said she was sexually promiscuous and would sleep with any man who wanted her. He seemed to revile her. He never seemed to realize that, when he was describing *her*, he was also describing himself.

Regardless of what had taken place in John's childhood, *I* was the one who was suffering from the consequences. It wasn't an enviable position to be in, and I was losing strength each day that I remained in this toxic relationship.

PART II

The Search for My Identity

CHAPTER 7

Is There a Doctor in the House?

My marriage was not improving, and on a daily basis I was digging myself more and more into a rut. I no longer cared if John hit me. Sometimes, seeing his anger start to build, I would do something to bring him over the edge just to get it over with. There was always the "honeymoon phase" after he hit me, and I began to live for those times. My illness was growing stronger than his was.

It was not the physical or verbal abuse that finally made me seek help, but a phone call from my mother on my 42nd birthday. Her gift to me was a "blanket apology." She said if she had done anything to hurt me for the last 40-some years, she wanted me to forgive her.

I was dumbfounded. I always thought an apology was the opportunity for us to express what we had done wrong. So I questioned her: "Where is this coming from, Mom? I don't understand."

My mother then began to tell me that she understood what made me turn out the way I did. Then, what had started out as an apology turned into insults. She was telling me all my faults and what created them. Happy birthday!

I didn't know what to say, so I told her I accepted her "gift." Then, I spent the remainder of the day trying to understand her call. I was tired of being confused, of being told I was wrong and what was wrong with me. Finally, I called a friend and asked for the name of a good psychologist. I had just about had it with my life.

Therapy wasn't going to be easy for me, though. As a lifelong pleaser, I didn't want anyone—not even a therapist—to think ill of me. It had always been difficult for me to talk about things that really troubled me. I felt it was a weakness to show pain or hurt, and I could never understand how some of my friends could cry and act vulnerable. Instead, I had grown accustomed to covering up my feelings with anger or apathy.

I finally did make the appointment, though, thank God.

Dr. Bob Mosby, my therapist, reminded me of a college professor: tall and thin, with penetrating but kind eyes. His office was lined with shelves full of books, and any of them could be borrowed and read. Between his chair and the sofa I sat on, he had a small table with different items on it to pick up and touch or play with while you talked. It helped make me comfortable.

I told Bob I was in a new marriage and having difficulty adapting. I also told him of my mother's phone call. He gathered background on my family and me, and the hour seemed to fly by. It wasn't until he asked me if I wanted to come back for another appointment and was checking his calendar that I finally began to open up.

Almost as an afterthought, I said, "By the way, my new husband is beating me." I sounded casual, but it was *extremely* difficult for me to say those words.

Bob turned in his chair to face me. Looking over the top

of his glasses, he said, "Yes, I do think we need to talk again."

John thought that I was going to a counselor because of my mother. He was an ally in my problems with her. Not appreciating women for anything but their role as sexual objects, it was only natural. He told me that he thought my mother was flirting with him on more than one occasion, which I know was wishful thinking on his part. During this point in my life, I didn't care.

I had stopped confiding in Debbie or Roberta, my closest friends, about John's abuse, because I was ashamed to still be with him. I knew they would always be there for me, but I didn't feel right dragging them into this mess.

Once, Debbie had forced me to go to the doctor after seeing bad bruises on my knees. John had thrown me through a door, and after hitting the wall on the other side of the door, I landed on the hard tile floor. My knees were swollen and black.

During my appointment, I finally told my doctor what was going on. "Di," he said, "I can't force you to leave your marriage. Only you can make that decision. I hope you think seriously about what is happening. I have a lot of female patients in the same boat as you, and I can tell you, it doesn't get any better."

Now, fearing for my life, I did decide to tell my sister what my marriage was really like. I told her that if anything happened to me to be sure John was investigated. She begged me to leave. I told her I was working on it but had to be careful. If nothing else, being able to confide in her deepened our relationship.

The most important clue that I was ready to get well

mentally was that it no longer mattered to me why John beat me—but I did need to know what had caused me to marry him and then stay with him after the first time he hit me. I guess I had grown tired of being the rescuer and trying to understand why other people did the things they did. I was now concerned about *me*.

Looking back, I realized that I had never been attracted to nice men. My former husband was not physically violent, but he was never around emotionally; I could never take problems to him. He told me at the end of our marriage that he wasn't able to be there for me because he couldn't even be around for himself on an emotional level. He admitted that he had never done anything for me unless he benefited from it himself. Afraid of intimacy, it seems fitting that I would marry a man who was incapable of being intimate.

The key to my attraction to these types of men seemed to lie not only in my low self-esteem and false beliefs about myself, but in the manner I had been raised by my parents. At 42 years of age, I wasn't going to blame all my problems on my mom and dad, but I had to understand what had happened that caused me to think the way I did and continually get involved with men who were emotionally vacant.

I had listened to audiocassettes and read books for years on self-esteem. Tapes played in my car as I drove to and from work, and I hooked myself up to a headset almost every night listening to those that held subliminal messages. But nothing changed. I was still plagued by self-doubt on a daily basis.

How could people learn to believe in their positive traits and actually realize them in their everyday lives? I had met many people who could quote what the self-help books said but still didn't seem to be able to truly believe, feel, or live the truths they had read or heard. It seemed hopeless.

I contemplated suicide regularly. I was so tired of feeling the way I had my entire life. Although I had accomplished some very exciting things in my life and had won impressive awards, none of these honors dispelled the belief that I was absolutely worthless.

The only reason I didn't take my own life was my children. My uncle had committed suicide, and our family had experienced so much grief as a result of this act. I believed that I didn't have the right to ruin my children's lives. Instead, I kept telling myself that there was a wonderful, happy life out there somewhere—where, I didn't know.

Bob, my therapist, had so much to sort through, but what I thought was an impossible task never seemed to frustrate him. He just continued to listen and gave advice when I asked for it.

I was so confused when I began to see Bob. I had chosen a male counselor because, if I had seen a female therapist and she told me it was wrong for a man to hit a woman, I would have convinced myself she was telling me that because she was a woman. I had to hear it from a man. I needed a man's perspective to tell me that my life was not normal. I also believe, because of my upbringing, that I didn't truly trust other women. And yet, although having a man's approval was very important to me, I secretly held men in contempt. I never dated nice men for very long because I claimed I found them boring. I had always said I needed a challenge. What I really needed was a man who would fulfill my father's opinion of me: a woman who was not worthy of anything or anyone that was positive or appealing.

One time I dated a nice man for a short time and then "dumped" him. Every time he picked me up for a date, he brought 13 long-stemmed roses—12 would be one color, and the 13th, a different color. He said that the one rose represented me because I stood out in a crowd and was special.

He arranged for my son, Derek, and me to do exciting things and would send a car and driver to take us to these events. He drove me crazy! I didn't want a man who was always there giving me gifts. My friends laughed when I said he was too nice.

But, truthfully, the main reason I stopped seeing him was because the man I had dated before him, who was verbally abusive and a real jerk, had started calling me again and I wanted to date him. So that's what I did until his abuse got to be too much to handle and I stopped seeing him. But I still had no desire to date the nice man.

I didn't have a clue how to have a healthy relationship with a man. I'd never been close to my father, my male role model. He had always yelled at me, and I can't remember him ever giving me a single compliment.

During one session, Bob explained, by marrying John, I had basically married my father because their personalities were very similar. My father was verbally abusive while I was growing up and even continued in this pattern into my adult years. Subconsciously, I thought that if I could get John to love me and treat me well, it would be the same as having my father finally love me and treat me with respect.

There was one catch, though: I had married a man who not only didn't know how to love, but who actually hated women. I had set myself up for failure. I was swimming against the tide and sinking.

Doors to my lost memories were slowly opening, though. I recalled the first time John had beaten me and the ride home from the party, when we had left so abruptly. In his car, when he was screaming at me, the familiar feeling I had felt was exactly the same as when I would get in a car with my dad, who often chose a vehicle as a battleground. This was an enclosed space in which I was literally a captive audience to his verbal tirades.

As the memories flooded back to me, I remembered road trips with my parents. I could see as clearly as if I were still in the car with them, my father driving and looking back at me, screaming about something that had enraged him. Every time we drove home from a restaurant, he would be yelling at the top of his lungs about some imagined offense I had committed while eating.

My therapist was correct—I had indeed married my father when I married John. Bob told me that he thought I should confide in my parents that John was abusing me, but I really fought him on this point. Finally, and very reluctantly, I gave in.

I called my mother from the store one morning. After delaying the inevitable with small talk, I got to the point. "Mom, listen, I have to tell you something." She waited for me to continue. I had to get it over with.

"I don't think John and I are going to make it. He's not the man I thought he was. He's been beating me and has really hurt me. I'm scared of him, and as soon as I can do it safely, I'm going to leave him. I just needed to tell you." There. It was done. I held my breath.

"Oh dear." She seemed to want to end our conversation, so I didn't try to drag it on any longer. I didn't hear from my parents for a week.

Finally, my father called me at the store. "Your mother told me about your call."

My heart pounded as I waited for him to continue. I should explain that anytime I heard my father's voice on the phone, I was instantly filled with dread and apprehension. His calls were never uplifting, only condemning.

"Here you go again, causing trouble. First of all, I don't like you calling your mother and upsetting her."

I wanted to choke Bob and myself for opening this can of worms. "But Dad, she's my mother. Aren't daughters supposed to go to their moms if they have a problem?" I could feel the tears burning in the back of my eyes. This was more pain that I could do without.

His voice took on the familiar tone of hatred that he continually directed toward me. "You always have a problem. *You* are a problem, always have been. I spent four days on John's boat with him, and I can tell you that he is not a violent man. I would have seen some sign of it if he was."

Thinking I needed to defend myself, I answered, "Well, he hid it from me for four months, so what's four days to him?"

"You've brought this on yourself. I don't want you calling your mother anymore, understand?" So much anger—he was always so furious with me.

His words hurt so much that I started to cry. "Okay, Dad, I won't call again."

He wasn't finished. "Another thing, your mother called you on your birthday and asked you for forgiveness. Not once during that entire conversation did you apologize to her and ask her forgiveness for the things that you've done to hurt her."

Wait a minute! This was too much. He was talking foolishness. I had repeatedly had scripture thrown at me as far back as I could remember. I, too, read the Bible and knew what it said. Besides my pain, I was feeling righteous indignation!

"I think you better read the Bible you always quote to me, Dad. It says not to ask for forgiveness expecting anything in return."

I don't believe he heard what I said, or at least he pretended not to. He had a habit of mumbling the whole time I spoke—his way of not listening.

"You should have begged your mother for forgiveness!" he yelled. Then he hung up on me. End of conversation.

My sister, Gail, ended up telling me what had really happened regarding the birthday call. My mother evidently wasn't having a particular prayer answered. The Bible states that sometimes if another person has a grudge against you, then you need to talk with that person and ask for forgiveness. Once that is out of the way, your prayer will be answered.

That was the self-serving reason she had called. It had nothing to do with me at all.

Bob and I were just beginning to delve into many of the problems between my father and me. I remembered a time when I was 27 years old and was visiting my parents for the weekend. I was riding in the car with my father, and as usual, we got into an argument. I suddenly asked him, "You don't like me, do you?"

He answered without even a slight pause. "I didn't like you the day you were born, I don't like you now, and I won't like you when you die." There was the truth—put out into the universe to cause me great pain. But the pain was never enough to keep me away or stop me from trying to gain his respect.

Also, I had heard my mother's words all my life as she spoke about having two children so close together. My sister was only 18 months older than I was. I finally asked her if I was an unwanted pregnancy. She told me, "Yes, you were. I didn't want another baby."

Now I had this new heartache to deal with, and I was furious with Bob, believing that he had caused me unnecessary pain. I told him so during our next session.

"I tried to warn you, Bob. My parents don't like to talk to me, let alone hear about my problems. They've never stood behind me emotionally, and they didn't this time either."

As always, Bob sat across from me with his hands under his chin. He let me blow off steam until I finally wore down, but when he spoke, his words brought about a new understanding.

"I'm sorry you had to experience this hurt, but there's a reason for it."

Why? So I could feel even worse about myself than I already did?

"You have to understand that you continue to do the same things over and over and think that somehow you will get different results."

I had heard that somewhere before: *To continue in the same pattern and expect different results was a definition of insanity*. Was I insane?

Bob continued, "How many times in your life have you gone to your parents and asked for help or advice and been refused?"

He had a point. "I can't recall them ever giving me support. My father has sometimes handed me money after the kids and I have visited them."

"Were strings attached to the money?" he asked.

I thought back to all the years that this very thing had happened. "Well," I recalled, "my father would always tell me not to spend it on clothing or things for myself. Just groceries or bills. He would also sort of hold it over my head. If I didn't act the way he liked, there was no money."

"So, the money wasn't really a gift. It could be called a reward for being a good girl or a punishment if it wasn't given?"

"But he loaned me the money to buy my business!"

With his usual wisdom, Bob explained, "Yes, and look at what's happened. You're now trying to prove your worth by working yourself to death, and you're even further indebted to him while being under his full control."

He continued to probe. "What about emotional support? Was it given to you?"

I really had to dig deep for these answers. "A few times. But usually if I was having some problem with one of the kids and would call for advice, I was simply told that they didn't have the answers."

"Even though you met the same response each time you called, did that stop you from calling?"

A light finally went off in my head! "No, it didn't."

Bob continued to sit across from me and study my face. "So, you've spent a lot of years repeating the same process while getting the same reactions. Why do you think you keep doing that?"

It was foreign for me to try and figure out why I did the things that I did. I had grown accustomed to other people telling me what to do and say. I was also used to covering up my true motives.

"I think if I'm correct, the reason I've continued to try to get their support is that it's important to me. It's natural for children, no matter what their age, to want their parents' support."

"Yes, that's true. What other reasons?"

"I thought that if my parents were able to help me, it might make them feel needed, a part of my life."

Bob just stared. He wasn't going to give me the answers. I had to find them myself. "I suppose the main reason would be to get their approval," I admitted.

Bingo! Bob's face lit up like a beacon. "Yes, that's right! But why is their approval so important to you?"

Suddenly, after so many years, I understood. "Because I've never had it."

We weren't finished. Bob asked, "Since you say you've never had your parents' approval and this appears to be a lifelong problem, what would make you believe that suddenly they would give it to you freely?"

Good question. I felt a sudden change in the pattern of my thoughts. It felt like a piece of cobweb had broken loose. There was an awareness that had not been there for 42 years! I could feel the wheels turning in my head.

I sat and stared at Bob while I thought. There were so many feelings flowing that I didn't even see his face. It was as though a movie was being played before my eyes of all the attempts and futile efforts performed by me to get two people to approve of my life and me.

"Oh my gosh, Bob! I *never* will have their approval. Even when my life was happy and great events were taking place, they didn't approve of me. It was almost like they wanted me to fail."

"So you're saying that, chances are, your parents will *never* approve?"

"That's right!"

Bob was as excited as I was. "Do you see now why it's so illogical to actively seek something that has never happened and probably never will?"

As I drove home, my mind was flooded with memories. I remembered all the times I'd bought my parents nice Christmas or birthday gifts that I really couldn't afford, waiting for some acknowledgment or show of thanks that never came. I recalled all the times I didn't act like my true self, instead trying to be what I *thought* they wanted me to be. And I relived many of the situations in which I would feel like a nervous wreck while in the same room with them, laughing and joking to cover my tension.

I remembered family pictures. My father always had a scowl on his face, and I believed it was because of me. I was so distasteful to him and made his life so miserable that I made him frown. If there was a family problem, I was somehow blamed for it. If my mother was ill, it was *my* fault.

I sure did think a lot of myself, causing all the problems in the universe!

Now I was repeating the same behavior with John. I believed that I provoked his anger and violence. I had taken it upon myself to accept all the shame, while he felt none. I continued to stay with John, but I expected different results. I would return to my childhood and respond like a little girl each time he grew angry—and for what? It never prevented me from being hit!

I had always acted like a child around my parents, thinking that this would make them back off and be kind to me. What would happen if I acted the way that I felt? It couldn't be any worse than what was already happening.

Obviously, it was time—at 42 years of age—to grow up!

CHAPTER 8

Light at the End of the Tunnel

Did I ever possess my own power? Just a small amount. Any firmness or strength that I showed openly was quickly taken away by my parents. Why? The key word is *control.*

Controlling types of people are actually very fearful. Once they feel that they are losing control over another person who has always submitted to their demands, they will either back down, try a different approach, or become more threatening.

I detested controlling types of people, yet I sought them out. I had the need to return to the familiar, and I associated control with love. It was all I knew. I was also a controlling person. I didn't try to control others with violence, but I did so with actions or self-pity. I wanted people to react to my games, not to the truth.

Because I seemed to have no control over my own life—in fact, I had given it away—I needed others to control me. Since I lacked a belief in myself, I sought approval from those who would tell me what I needed to hear—whether good or bad. But somehow I couldn't accept positive comments. Suspicious, I would wonder what those people wanted from me. They had to have an ulterior motive. However, I would readily accept any negative comments.

Bob held the key to my unfoldment, and each week, we slowly unlocked the door. The most important strategy became the most difficult: How could I get my own power back? I had a problem taking what was rightfully mine from the day of my birth. As a child, it was taken from me. As an adult, I gave it away. I only *thought* I had power!

What was causing my therapy to progress so slowly was John's continued abuse. I was learning about myself, but he was staying exactly the same. Bob feared that John might break my neck by picking me up by the throat and throwing me, and he begged me to seriously consider moving out of John's house.

Also, when my father would call me, it stalled my treatment. He knew I was seeing a therapist and would say, "I don't know why you bother; you aren't getting any better." It caused me to take several steps backward.

I finally decided to cut off all contact with my parents for a while. I didn't return the messages left on my answering machine, and my employees answered the phone for me and told my father I would call him back, but I didn't. Since we didn't talk very often, it didn't create problems.

Bob had to try to erase my negative beliefs about myself, but it was an agonizing task and took many months. He told me that my father couldn't know what made me tick and wasn't privy to my thoughts and feelings. He said that my father knew no more about me than a stranger on the street, but I found that hard to believe. He was my father! He had spent the first 18 years of my life with me, so surely he knew me better than anyone!

Bob explained, "What your father told you about yourself is what he wanted you to believe. Every negative affirmation that was fed into your mind was put there to keep you under his control—to beat you down, so to speak."

If Bob was correct, I wasn't stupid, lazy, worthless, and ugly—all those things I had believed my whole life.

But then, who and what was I? I had never met the real me. As I started to absorb and understand Bob's words, this new person began to form. All those books and tapes that I had read and listened to couldn't do it, but now it was really beginning to happen. For the first time in my life, I had a small glimmer of healthy self-esteem. And along with it came power.

I noticed that I began to avoid negative people. I was aware of how destructive negativity could be. I no longer wanted to speak or think negative words or thoughts. A new awareness was taking place, which was much easier and caused less stress.

I had a new love for my fellow human beings as I started to see others for the way they were. Maybe one of my customers had been in an argument with her husband that morning and was taking it out on my employees. Perhaps she was angry as a result of the way her life had turned out. There could be many reasons, but her actions didn't have to affect my life or ruin my day.

I felt a true happiness begin to grow deep inside my soul. This was something that no person could take from me. The real me, who had been hidden, disguised, and ruled over for so many years, was actually pretty cool. I liked her.

With Bob's help, I came to many new realizations. One of these occurred during a "homework" assignment that he gave me. I was to sit quietly where I wouldn't be disturbed and envision myself in a calm setting. Then I was to think of all my positive qualities. If I started to drift toward negative thoughts, I was to end the exercise.

I must have been like a volcano ready to erupt, because

the first time I tried the visualization, I had an awareness that was to change my life. As I tried to think of good qualities I might have, the word *kind* came to my mind. I started to laugh. "Kind? I'm not kind."

Then, something happened that I had never experienced before. A voice came through so clear and strong that I thought a person must have walked into the room and was speaking to me. It said, "No, Di, you are a very kind person, but you have your kindness so hidden by anger that it can't be seen."

How can I explain a heavy weight that threatened to kill me, suddenly being lifted? I felt as if I could really breathe for the first time. In a flash, I realized that *anger was a choice,* and nothing else. If another person harmed me or perpetrated some action upon me that was not right, it was up to me to be angry or let it slide. Anger was very draining. I had felt drained all my life. I had never known anything else—but I always felt that I was sad, not angry.

What I thought was strength was actually my greatest limitation. I had falsely believed that to show sorrow or pain was weak; to express anger would make me feel and look stronger. I became aware of feelings and emotions I had never felt before. Evidently, this was a crucial yet dangerous point in my therapy. Bob insisted I come in "as needed" while experiencing these feelings.

I began to laugh freely and have fun. I had always been a cheerful, joking person, but this was different. Looking back, I think that before my therapy, my laughter was actually near hysteria and was a mask to cover all my pain and shame. But now, my laughter was genuine and came from my heart, and it was very healing.

Unlike most victims of domestic violence, I was receiving therapy while I continued to live with my abuser. The only reason John didn't object was because he thought I was seeking help for my problems with my parents. After only several months of Bob's help and guidance, I started to understand that I was never going to change John.

Although John's verbal and physical abuse continued, my response had changed. He was expecting me to behave in a certain way—the same way I had always reacted when he would try to pick a fight. This would perpetuate the cycle. I would react, he would grow angry, and the fight was on! When my actions changed because I knew what he was attempting to do, it threw him off balance. He wasn't sure how to respond. He would then try harder to make me angry. It was very uncomfortable, but the cruel verbal assaults no longer hurt me.

The truth is, John was responsible for his behavior, and I was responsible for mine. I would never believe negative remarks made about me by another person again—especially by those who didn't live a loving life themselves.

The Bible says, "Ye shall know the truth and the truth shall set you free." How true. I was learning about the true woman hidden deep inside. There was a great freedom in that. For the first time, I truly believed that God loved me.

Although I was beginning to understand my own actions and reactions, another person was involved that was being hurt by John's conduct. Derek had just turned 12 and was able to see that something was amiss in the family structure. He didn't have to be a rocket scientist to tell that things weren't right when he returned at the end of the summer. John had always worked with Derek on batting and pitching or basketball, but what had once been kindness and tolerance was now irritation and unrealistic expectations.

Once when Derek used the wrong terminology about some sport, John jumped all over him. I was furious and told John, "Don't you ever speak to my son like that! You better remember how you felt when your stepfather spoke to you that way."

But strangely, he denied that his stepfather was a bad guy. "My stepfather wasn't mean to me. He was a very nice man."

Was he deaf and blind, or did he suffer from amnesia? I replied, "From what I've heard about that man, he was a jerk." John didn't answer. I have no idea what he was thinking, but I knew I was not going to allow him to treat my son unkindly.

Although John didn't seem to be the jealous type when other men looked at me, and he still tried to make me talk about previous lovers during sex, he was insanely jealous of my former husband, Derek's father. My ex was not allowed in the house when he stopped by to pick up Derek for an outing, and he was treated rudely when he telephoned the house to speak with his son. It was so childish, but the horrible part was how it made Derek feel. He was caught in the middle and didn't deserve to be there. The tension in our home was so thick that you could cut through it with a butter knife. I had grown weary of pretending that all was well on the home front.

Then, one evening, John was backing me down the hall when I tripped on the rug and fell backward. Derek was in his bedroom nearby, studying. When he heard the commotion, he opened his bedroom door. There I was, lying on my back in the middle of the hall with John standing over me. I saw my son's face, but I couldn't think of any excuse or lie. John walked away, and I stood up and walked to the laundry room, leaving Derek standing there. My poor son.

Later, when Derek and I were alone, he asked me what was going on. I played innocent. "Nothing. I fell on the rug." He looked at me, disbelieving.

"No, really, Derek. I fell backward when I caught the heel of my shoe on the rug. John just happened to be there, seeing if I was okay."

As he walked away, he said, "Whatever, but I don't believe you. I can feel in my heart that something isn't right." Out of the mouths of babes . . .

Trying to pretend in front of Derek that my marriage was a happy one became a chore. I was tied in knots, acting chatty and smiling. John knew it was extremely important to me to protect my son from any type of emotional distress. He used my concern as a threat against me. If I didn't do what he expected, he would tell me he was going to hit me in front of Derek.

I constantly had stomach pains. The shelf above my desk at the store contained antacids, aspirin, and stress-tab vitamins; and I was also taking an antidepressant that my doctor had prescribed for me. I was a walking medicine cabinet. I was not only covering up by denying and pretending, but I was masking my health deterioration with medicine.

Believe it or not, though, I was trying to live a "normal" life. John, Derek, and I would go on weekend camping and fishing trips, and John usually behaved while around Derek. Of course, I was turning myself inside out to keep everyone happy.

There were times when John would actually act like a nice guy. He was not angry *all* the time. I just never knew what would set him off. It could be alcohol one time, but the next time, he would erupt even when he was completely sober.

Then, Derek decided he wanted a dog. I thought it was a good idea. I believe every boy should have a pet to teach him how to care and love another being. It's sort of a training process for the day he might become a father.

Previously we had owned a Doberman. We loved that breed, but John didn't want a large dog, and frankly, we didn't have enough room. John agreed to let Derek get a dog as long as it was a breed he approved of. He decided on a wire-haired fox terrier.

This dog was a nut. So much energy! Derek named her "Oreo" because of the black markings on her back, which resembled the cookie. She was a source of entertainment. Each night, she curled up beside Derek's head, sharing his pillow with him.

Sometimes there may be an event that takes place that may not be related to anything in particular but will cause you to become aware of something that is very important in understanding yourself. An incident with the dog did just that.

Derek had left for school, and I was getting ready for work. John was angry about something and started throwing his usual temper tantrum. I ignored him and continued to apply my makeup. Oreo was standing beside me. Suddenly, John tried to kick the dog. She was fast and managed to dodge his foot, and he kicked a hole in the wall.

Oreo had been trained not to go out the front door, as there was no fence and she could run into the street and get hit by a car. As I continued to ignore John and began brushing my hair, I heard him open the front door and call the dog.

"Di, I'm throwing your dog out the front door. If she gets hit by a car, it will be your fault." What an idiot!

I began putting my makeup and brush away and grabbed my jacket and walked out the door. When I had backed my car out of the garage, I saw John standing there, holding the dog. He was smiling and pointing to her.

"Look, I found your dog! She's okay." He actually believed that I should be thankful that he had rescued her, after he was the one who had put her in danger! I just shook my head and drove off.

I was livid, although I didn't allow John to see it. How dare he try to harm an innocent little dog. She was helpless and a victim of his insanity. But then my mouth dropped open with shock!

I thought, *Wait a minute—you're furious that he would try to kick a dog, but you don't get that angry when he kicks you!* Apparently, I thought more of a dog's rights than my own. Just where was my self-worth, anyway?

I weighed 120 pounds, but John was a foot taller and nearly 100 pounds more. I didn't stand any more of a chance against John than the dog did!

John had told me on more than one occasion that if I tried to leave him, he would make sure that I lost custody of Derek. He sometimes would refer to Derek and me as Oedipus Rex, referring to a sexual relationship. So I had to worry about what he might try to do to harm my relationship with my son, along with what he might do to me.

When Derek left to visit his father for spring break, something inside me began to stir and say, "It's now or never. Get out of here while Derek is gone."

I started leaving my store in the afternoon to look for an apartment, and I found a nice two-bedroom place close to Derek's school and the store. Although it was located only a mile from John's house, it was safer than living with him. I signed a six-month lease, but now I had to find the right time to move without endangering my life.

I believe in prayer, so that's what I did. I prayed for God to step in and create some kind of situation that could get me out of John's house. It happened sooner than I expected.

John would sometimes call me a very demeaning and degrading name. It hurt deeply, and I knew that no man, especially a husband, should ever call a woman this "name." I finally told him that if he ever called me that again, we were history. He must have felt that I was serious because he refrained from using the word, even in fits of anger.

Then, one evening, I went to bed early after an especially grueling day at work. All I wanted was to read for a few minutes in bed before sleeping.

As usual, John was angry about something and started yelling insults from the living room sofa. I ignored him. His verbal assault continued and grew more heated. I continued to read my book and didn't answer him. He walked into the bedroom, and very deliberately, he called me the "name."

Strangely, when beating, kicking, choking, or spitting in my face had not been the straw that broke the camel's back, calling me that horrible name finally did it.

I looked at him over my book and said in a calm, level voice, "You have just screwed up. You have ended this marriage."

My heart never skipped a beat, and I felt no fear. I could tell from his facial expression that this time it was different. I was no longer making empty threats.

I looked down and continued reading my book. He stood for a moment staring at me and then quietly left the room. He slept on the sofa that night. I believe he actually feared me.

I called the moving company the next morning and set the upcoming Saturday as my moving day.

Freedom at last.

CHAPTER 9

Misdirected Ego

I proudly told myself that John would be the only one to suffer the consequences of what he had done. I was very wrong. My pain was not finished.

Oreo and I stayed at Roberta's house until my moving day arrived. The dog worked on destroying her home, chewing up everything she could find. I left a message on John's answering machine, telling him that I would be at his house Saturday morning with the movers.

I warned him against destroying any of my property and also told him that should he choose to become violent, I would call the police and have him arrested, which I should have done long ago. He tried to call me at the store several times, but I refused to speak with him.

Bright and early Saturday morning, I met the movers in front of John's house. He was there, acting sad and docile, and asked me if I would sit down in the kitchen and talk to him. We had a cup of coffee while the movers went about their work.

"Please don't do this. Couples never work out problems while they're separated. Give us another chance." But his remorseful looks no longer worked on me.

"No, John. You've had more than enough time to stop the horrible things that you do. You say that you're sorry, but nothing changes. I can't live like this."

I just wanted to get the hell out of that house where I had suffered so much pain and sorrow. I thought of some religions that burned pure, white candles in homes like this to rid it of evil spirits. This place was in dire need of candles!

He was begging. "Di, I can change. Honest. Just give me the chance to prove it to you!"

I let out a long sigh. I had stopped smoking, but I could have *eaten* a cigarette at that point!

"Listen, John, if you could change, why didn't you try to do it after you beat me the first time? Why do you suddenly feel the need for change now when I've finally reached my limit and am leaving you?"

Once again, I was trying to reach him and make him see the pain he had caused. Somewhere, deep in my heart, I felt that there was still a chance of him miraculously seeing the light. I was also trying to thwart his anger.

He hung his head like a boy who was being disciplined. As I looked at him, I realized that I no longer found him attractive. The person I had once considered one of the most handsome men I had ever seen—this gorgeous male model—was ugly and pathetic.

If he was trying to use this humble act to win me over, he was making a mistake. Looking at him trying to pretend he was feeling something he wasn't capable of nauseated me. Now, the tide had turned. *I* found *him* distasteful.

I continued to talk, wishing the movers would hurry. "John, let me try to explain something to you. This is more about me than it is about you. I am in search of inner peace. You can't stop it by hitting me or being nice. It's for me and no other person. I know if I stay with you, I'll still find that peace, but it would delay the process."

I have to be honest about my thoughts at this time. I didn't actually care if he understood. Very rarely did John listen to what I had to say. It was a good opportunity to show him what I felt without being hit.

He sat and listened.

"Sometimes two personalities don't gel, no matter what is done to try and make it happen. We have always argued and will continue to do so. That is not what I want for my life. I'm at the age where I want peace, happiness, and tranquillity."

I thought back to the time when he hit me in the head with his coffee mug. I didn't want to get the movers involved in a domestic scene. I was prepared to jump and run for the door. Many times when I felt John was cool and calm, he would unexpectedly go into a rage.

John just sat in the chair. His voice took on the little-boy quality that was trying to understand what I felt. "You really have changed. I've watched it happening. You won't yell back and defend yourself. You don't seem to be bothered by anything I do. I think you just don't care about me anymore."

It was clear that John was having a pity party and was trying to get me to join in. He was also trying to get me to say something to make him feel good about himself, while causing me to fall back into the same old dance. But I had changed the song on the jukebox and was dancing to a different beat.

I refused to reply to his foolish statement, but just sat in my chair and looked at him in silence. He realized that his strategy wasn't working, so it was time for him to move on to something new.

"Would you do something for me? Will you promise me that you won't file for a divorce until I have the chance to get help?"

Now this was getting interesting.

"If you don't object and your therapist will agree to it, I will see him," John told me. "He seems to have helped you so much; maybe he can help me."

Was he serious? I leaned back in my chair and examined this man, this stranger I had been married to for just a little over a year.

He continued with his plan. "If I miss any appointments with Bob, I will give him permission to call you and tell you. That way you'll know if I'm serious about getting well."

The movers were signaling me that they were ready to leave. As I stood up to leave, I looked down at John. "Okay, I won't file for a divorce yet. But I will not see you or live with you."

He began to object.

"My rules this time, John. Not yours."

With those words, his reign of terror and control were over. I didn't care if he saw Bob or didn't see him. I was busy and broke from moving and renting the apartment and didn't have the time or money to retain a lawyer. A divorce wasn't at the top of my list. Getting away from his threats and beatings was what mattered.

As I drove away in my car, with the moving van following me, all I could say was, "Thank you, Jesus."

During the next few weeks, I realized I was having fun for the first time in years. My apartment was strictly female except for Derek's bedroom. I purchased pink-flowered dishes, pink glassware, pink-handled silverware, and pink napkins—a bit extreme, but understandable after living in John's masculine house with its dark, boring colors, which I was not allowed to change.

I decided to go into a little debt and bought a white wicker bedroom set. As far back as I could remember, I had always wanted one. I bought a white lace bedspread. No man alive would have felt at home in this apartment.

I called Derek from the store and told him that we had a different phone number at home. I wanted to see him in person and not explain everything over the phone. Deep down, I was ashamed that I had made such a stupid decision and married John, plus I had uprooted Derek again. I also feared he might decide to stay with his father. I was still thinking of myself and my needs instead of Derek's. I had a lot of growing up to do.

I continued my sessions with Bob. I knew John was seeing him, but we never spoke of it. I was there to work on myself, not John. John would call me at home periodically, feeling sorry for himself. He told me he was severely depressed and was feeling suicidal. I finally told Bob what he was saying. He simply replied in a bored tone, "Really? If he is, he hasn't mentioned it to me." We never mentioned John again.

My youngest daughter, Brandi, stayed with me off and on—mostly on. She had graduated from high school and was ready to be on her own, but she was doing it in baby steps. She worked at my store and was a wonderful employee. She was struggling to find her way in the adult world. The more she had seen of John, the less she had liked him. She had always tried to avoid him when he was working with me.

Because I had been so isolated by John's opinions, I now realized that his attitude about my family had created barriers. Little by little, I learned of different incidents.

Brandi didn't tell me until after I moved out that once when John had given her a ride home from work, he became angry and began yelling at her. She said he was in her face, threatening her. But she didn't tell me what happened for fear of causing problems in what had seemed to be a happy marriage. She simply told me that she was going to stay with her girlfriend who had just rented an apartment.

Not suspecting what had taken place and thinking she wanted to be on her own, I said, "Okay, honey."

My oldest daughter, Leisa, had a son, Nicholas, who was the joy of my life. I was crazy about this baby and when Leisa would ask "Grandma" to baby-sit, I was thrilled. But John made me so miserable, complaining about dirty diapers, spit-up, and crying that I soon stopped taking care of him. It created too many problems.

Leisa's husband, Dennis, was a sweet, gentle, and kind young man who worked for me as the night manager. John had told me that he thought Dennis was stealing from me, but I refused to believe him.

"But the registers are short this morning," he would say. Then the following morning, the register would be over the same amount that they had been short the previous day.

I told John, "Obviously you made a mistake counting the money."

Never one to give in, he explained that Dennis had probably taken the money and then changed his mind and put it back. I would roll my eyes in disbelief.

As I mentioned before, John insisted that my mother was flirting with him. He told me he thought my sister was a lesbian, as if this was sinful and would make me stay away from her. He never gave up. And in the end, his accusations and complaints *did* serve to reduce the time I spent with my family.

It's a common pattern in domestic violence situations: In order to have more control over his victim, the abuser will ridicule his wife's friends or be rude to them when they call or visit. He discourages her from talking to her friends on the phone.

He also begins to work on her family. He doesn't want to attend family gatherings and makes his wife feel guilty if she goes without him. If he does go, he's distant, and she must live with the consequences after they go home. Soon the friends and family grow weary of his behavior and stay away. By keeping her isolated and alone, there is no outside force to help her see what's wrong with her marriage.

Gradually, the abuser makes her his ally against those who were once her friends. Alone, with no one to turn to but her abuser, she begins to relate to him in the same manner in which a hostage will relate to her captor, given enough time. It is a mixture of brainwashing and survival—a very strong and effective combination.

Because I had started therapy, I was able to see what John was attempting to do. How could he dislike every single friend I had? I could also see that my children were losing respect for me for being with this antisocial, abusive man.

Derek returned from his spring vacation in time to start school, but one of John's predictions did come true: Derek was very unhappy. There had been too much change in his young life. I had once again uprooted him. Although we were only a mile away from John's house, this was a new neighborhood. Also, my son had been brought up in a small town and didn't like living in a large city.

Of course, I figured his father had been talking to him, too. It was only natural that Derek's father wanted him to live with him. It was the reasoning behind it that bothered me, though. He saw Derek as a piece of property that could be used to get even with me. He was still angry about the divorce. What I feared was Derek wanting to leave. I knew his father hated paying child support and worked on his vulnerable mind each time Derek visited him. Derek and I had always been so close that I didn't believe his father could talk him into moving.

When I came home from work one evening, Derek told me that he wanted to go live with his father because he just wasn't happy. I cried and tried to shame him with a guilt trip. It didn't work. He left.

I was hysterical. I was angry. I was hurt.

"Oh God, what have you done? My baby . . ." Of course, as soon as my father heard the news, he called me to tell me that Derek was better off with his father. I hung up on him.

I called a friend whom I always considered very wise and told him my sad tale of woe. I wanted him to join me in my lamenting.

He immediately responded. "So? That's your son's life, and he has a right to make a decision about his happiness. What does that have to do with you?"

I was hurt by his response. "But a son belongs with his mother!"

"Who says?"

I didn't have an answer. Who *did* say that? Some *mother?* I hadn't exactly thought of my son's welfare, only mine.

My friend began to soften a little. "Di, I know you hurt right now, but it's time to be honest with yourself. You know Derek's dad loves him and will take care of him. You work a lot of hours, and it isn't fair to him. If you will really think about it, what is hurt right now is your ego."

Thank God for reasonable friends. He gave me a lot to think about. I began to examine my motives that night, and I realized that almost everything I did was motivated by my ego. My ego wanted Derek with me, but it wasn't his happiness or well-being that had been the driving force. Of course I loved him, but doesn't love mean allowing a person to do what is right for him? I had put him through a lot because of my own needs and desires. For example, when I refused to call the police for help after John had beaten me, it was my ego that stopped me from calling. I didn't want my neighbors to know what was happening.

Now, my ego didn't want others to think I was such a horrible mother that my son had chosen to live with his father.

The list went on and on. I realized late in the night that ego was actually the opposite of love—the very thing I was seeking in my life. I would have to get my strong, temperamental ego out of the way before I could find inner peace. Realizing my problem became the first step.

I called Derek and told him I was sorry for my outburst. I loved him and always would. No more guilt trips. No more games and no more self-pity. I was getting there!

CHAPTER 10

Delving into the Truth

Am I psychic? No. My friends and I always tease, "Psycho perhaps, but not psychic!" If not, why did I continue to have the same dream about John even though I had left him? The same private detective brought me the same red folder with information about John, and I would still wake up before I knew what was in the folder. What was going on? What was in that dream that I needed to know? Should I hire a private investigator and check out his background? Why bother? I had already left him. But obviously in my subconscious, there was still some unfinished business.

I'd had dreams warning me of future events, but not about life-threatening situations. Why would I have the same dream when I was out of harm's way? Since I couldn't understand it, I ignored it.

I also experienced the most horrifying nightmares of John knocking on my door, and when I opened the door, he would be standing there, holding Oreo by the throat, choking her. It's terrifying enough to wake up from a dream like that, but being alone when I woke up really got to me. I would read late into the night until I fell asleep, only to have more nightmares. Soon I suffered from insomnia. I was exhausted.

My therapy grew more intense. I began to learn more about myself and the influence my father had over me. My father believed the worst of everyone, including me. Through self-protection, I learned to keep a distance between other people and myself. But if I thought I was protecting myself by putting up walls, I was fooling myself.

If we encounter others, chances are that another person will someday hurt us. It's called life. If we have walls up all the time, suspecting pain and rejection, we might miss some very valuable friendships along the way.

Bob knew I trusted no one, and in one session we did an experiment with body language in his office. Opening the bottom drawer of his filing cabinet, he rested one foot on the drawer.

"Stand across the room, Di, and look at me."

I walked to the opposite side of the room and stood.

"Look where your arms are!" They were folded across my chest. "That is a sign of protection, covering yourself. And look what parts of your body you're covering. It is a sexual type of hiding, and you're also covering your heart." He told me to drop my arms.

I obeyed, and he immediately stopped me. "Now, look where your arms are."

I couldn't believe it! My hands were covering my crotch!

"Do you see what you're doing?" I nodded my head in agreement. "Now, I'm going to begin to slowly walk toward you. The moment you start to feel uncomfortable, I want you to tell me to stop."

Bob took his foot off the filing cabinet door.

"Stop!" I yelled.

He looked at me strangely. "Are you serious?" He didn't take another step.

I felt a little ashamed, but I was trying to be truthful. "Yeah, I'm dead serious. I felt my heart beat faster, and I began to get a shy feeling."

He asked me to sit down, and then he leaned across the table toward me. "Di, do you think that I'm attracted to you in a sexual way?"

I went into a panic mode. This wasn't going to be one of these incidents I had heard about where the therapist makes a pass at his patient, was it?

"No, I don't think you're attracted to me." *Please God, don't let him be!*

He smiled. "You're right, I'm not. I'm dating a wonderful woman. I think you're a very pretty lady, but I don't desire you sexually."

I sat and stared at him. Why were we talking about this anyway? I shifted on the sofa.

He continued, "Look at me." Shyly, I met his stare. "Not every man who meets you wants something from you. Some men are just interested in talking to you and knowing you as a friend."

Really?

"I'll be honest with you. The first time I met you, I thought you were a nice person, but you only allowed me to reach out from a distance. You were so blocked and aloof, had it been a social event, I don't think it would have been worth the extreme effort to try and get to know you better."

There was silence. As always, Bob was going to make me get to the bottom of this problem.

"Why do you think you're this way?"

I had been in therapy long enough to know how to be honest with myself. Did others really see me as distant and aloof? I didn't feel that way inside. I always felt that I talked too much and gave away too much of myself—completely opposite of what Bob was saying.

Suddenly, there were tears, out of nowhere, flowing until I was sobbing hysterically. I couldn't turn them off! Breakthrough!

"Every time my father was angry with me or punished me, he told me I was sick and mentally ill. He called me crazy and told me I needed to have my head examined!" Where did this newfound knowledge come from?

I took the box of tissues Bob handed me, and continued.

"I've always believed if I allowed anybody to get close to me, they would find out that I was mentally ill. I've had a fear all my life that I'd end up in a hospital, drooling on myself in some corner."

Bob looked at me with compassion. "You carried this weight around with you all these years?"

It was a weight—a very heavy burden. It had been weighing me down most of my life. I nodded my head as I continued to cry.

"Di, you are *not* mentally ill."

I looked up, shocked. "I'm not?"

Bob reached over and took my hand in his. "No, you're not! Believe me, I have worked with many people who *are* truly mentally ill. You don't even come close. Perhaps, for whatever reason, your father felt that way about himself and was pushing it off on you. People will do that."

What followed was another drive home from the therapist with my mind racing and remembering! Everything was coming together. Besides relief, I was angry!

"How dare my father do that!" He had ruined a large part of my life, and for what? Here was a man who went to church every Sunday, watched nothing but Christian television—and told me what a sinner I was!

Did I want to call my father and tell him how I felt? No. I had learned, thanks to Bob, that sometimes things are better left unsaid. Would it change my father? Of course not. Our family was not one to work out problems. We only blamed.

I thought of the times when my mother or father would call and ask for "forgiveness." The problem in our family was there was never any sorrow for hurting each other. We never admitted we were wrong or irrational! We used the word *forgiveness* like something to be thrown around that was self-serving. If the other person wasn't willing to forgive, then he or she was the sinner.

When I analyzed John's apology or plea for forgiveness, the similarities astounded me! He would always begin with "I'm sorry," and that was always followed by "but." Then the reasons would be given as to why he had beaten me: I made him angry, I frustrated him, and I humiliated him.

It was interesting that I had continued in the same pattern with John as I had with my parents. Once the "apology" was given, I somehow would transfer all the blame for what had transpired onto myself. A human ricochet!

I also found it interesting that the church I had attended earlier in my life basically victimized its members, what I call "beating the flock." We were made to feel guilty and sinful if we didn't feel like forgiving another for some cruel deed. Therefore, we would say we forgave them, but we never truly felt it in our hearts. We were simply fearful of burning in hell for eternity.

I wasn't guiltless in all of my life circumstances either. I was at an age where I knew right from wrong, black from white, and what I *should* be doing with my life. I'm also not going to blame my parents for my misfortunes. They were repeating what my grandparents had taught them, and we were perpetuating a long chain of family dysfunction. I also repeated this behavior with other people. I blamed them for mistakes, criticized constantly, and felt rejected if they didn't accept my apology after I had hurt them.

As I continued with my philosophy on forgiveness, I was attempting to return to old habits that I knew, deep within my spirit, would harm me. I still needed to stay in contact with John—to be forgiving. To my way of rationalizing, he was working toward recovery, had seen the mistakes he'd made, and had almost lost a good woman. I felt I should offer him encouragement along his journey.

Although Bob had warned me about continuing to have periodic phone conversations with John, I saw no harm in them. John would call me once a week to tell me of his progress in therapy. He still begged me to hold off on divorce proceedings. He told me that I at least owed him that.

I remember thinking, *If I gave you what was owed to you right now, you would have a black eye, a sore crotch, a strained neck, and nightmares.*

I owed him a lot, but none of it was pleasant.

Besides going to Bob for therapy, Bob referred John to a support group for batterers. Trying to show me he was going to change, John attended weekly. I asked him what it was like and what they talked about.

"We have a group facilitator who leads the sessions. He tells us how stupid we are for hitting women because we'll never win. She'll call the police, and we'll end up in jail."

I wasn't exactly a picture of mental health myself, but I had to ask myself what good it did to tell these men this? How was that teaching them to control their anger or even get to the source of it? They were talking about consequences, not reasons. If you don't understand why you're doing something that is not only destructive but against the law, how could you change?

Most of the men in the group did not see themselves as abusers. To them, a man who came home after drinking all night and beat his wife for no reason was a batterer. If you hit a woman to keep her in line, it was acceptable. Neither John nor the other men felt they had done anything wrong. The conversations I had with John have always prohibited me from openly and eagerly suggesting the name of a batterer's support group to victims who contact me for help.

Consider this: It took me more than two years of intense counseling and soul searching to understand the part I had played in the domestic violence cycle—such as staying, and believing that I deserved the abuse. How could a man who has controlled and beaten his spouse for years, stop after a few sessions?

CHAPTER 11

Trying to Return to Familiar Territory

There is a story about a snake, which serves as a metaphor for needing help and seeking therapy. Before therapy, you are walking down a road. You see a snake lying in the road and pick it up and begin to play with it, but being a snake, it bites you.

During therapy, you are walking down this same road and see the snake again. You kick at it with your shoe and sort of play with it, but you don't pick it up. You've learned through experience that it will bite you.

At the end of therapy, you are once again walking down this same road and, as before, you see the same snake. This time, you cross to the other side of the road, avoiding it.

The National Clearinghouse for Battered Women states that a battered woman will leave her abuser seven times before she finally ends the relationship for good. Only battered women can understand why they do this, and even then, it's hard to formulate a response that makes sense. It's extremely difficult to break free of old habits and thought patterns. I was no different.

It had been three months since I'd moved out of John's house, and I was in the middle of therapy. I was so proud of myself for opening doors and learning new, healthy ways of dealing with problems. Why was I pulled back to the snake in the road, tempting it to bite me again?

In looking back at my reasons for the actions (which I will describe in just a moment), it is very important for me to be honest for the sake of all battered women. That is why I write about this. I cannot and will not deceive you or myself with excuses. Truth and honesty are the only keys to getting well.

Was I lonely? Perhaps, just a little. But I had work to keep me busy, and children to talk to and spend time with. So that really wasn't a valid reason.

Was I bored? Not really. I went to clubs, plays, shows, and parties with my girlfriends and male friends. I had a fairly busy social life.

Was it a need for sex? Definitely not. I tend to become very focused on things, such as my work, and when I do, I am not a sexual creature. If I had any sexual stirrings, there were a number of men I could have seduced (it isn't that difficult, you know) plus, with AIDS, I would have preferred self-gratification when desperate!

Did I feel the need to be with a man and still seek his approval? I don't think so. I was becoming more secure with myself and usually only sought my own approval. I enjoyed not having to answer to anybody. If I wanted to go someplace, I just grabbed my purse and went.

Okay then, why? Why did I allow myself to get sucked back into this black hole, so to speak, that I knew would bring me only harm and absolutely no good? Here comes the absolute, 100 percent truth:

1. Although I was still trying to get my ego out of the way, it would, at times, rear its ugly head. After five years, I was still trying to "one-up" Derek's father. I had an opportunity to outdo him in the "exciting parent" department—what is known as being a Disneyland Parent.

2. I still suffered from abandonment issues regarding Derek choosing to live with his father. I wanted him to be aware of just what he was missing when he chose to move out of my apartment, so I presented an opportunity to him that I *knew* he wouldn't be able to resist. I, being the great person that I am, went straight for his young and vulnerable heart, God, forgive me.

3. I had not grown or progressed nearly as far as I thought I could. Like an overweight person who has successfully lost some weight, but returns to old eating habits, I wasn't as strong as I convinced myself I was. Subconsciously, I wanted to return to my old habits. I was about to return to what was familiar. There was something deep inside my soul and spirit, if not my heart, that needed to do this.

Was I trying to self-destruct? Was there some part of me that still didn't love the true woman I was just beginning to find and know? In a way, yes. Remember that I had spent 42 years with self-hatred. I still didn't really believe that I deserved good things or love. Inside my mind, there was still more self-loathing than self-loving.

You know those devices called bug zappers? They are

electrical gadgets that create a purple light to attract insects. The insect is drawn to the light, and ZAP! It gets killed.

John was the purple light, and I was attracted to it. I still needed to fulfill my father's prophecy of me: "You will never amount to anything. You are worthless." The moth was flying into the flame again.

As I mentioned, Bob repeatedly warned me against having conversations with John, even though he too was in therapy. He warned me to just stay away—to have no contact, even by phone. But I didn't feel that it could do any harm. What damage could phone conversations cause? Plenty. The only way I know how to describe it is, if you're having a problem with heroin, you don't keep a dose of it in a syringe, ready to shoot up. It makes it too difficult to pass up the temptation.

My problem was no different from that of a drug addict. I seemed to be addicted to feeling bad about myself and being with those who would enforce this belief.

The incident I've been referring to up till now started innocently, with a phone call from John.

"Di, I was wondering if you'd be interested in going to the lake for a few days of fishing, tanning, and relaxation. I know you've been working a lot of hours and haven't taken a day off in a long time."

I had told him before that I would not see him socially. The thought of being alone with him in the middle of a very large lake was frightening. But, as if he was reading my thoughts, he continued, "Not alone with just the two of us. I thought you might want to invite Derek to come along. I know how much he loves sailing and fishing."

That was very true. When we had gone boating before and I would go below to fall into bed, Derek and John would remain on the upper deck with their poles hanging off the back of the boat, talking and laughing late into the night.

See how easy it is to slip back into the familiar? Our mind plays tricks on us. In just a few short months, I had forgotten the cruel words and painful blows. I forgot the fear and desire to escape. I remembered the good times at the lake and was turning my back on the important lessons I had learned in therapy. Why? Because it was easier than trying to continue to change. The ostrich was sticking its head back in the sand.

I also *needed* to believe that John had changed. He had seen the error of his ways and felt the sorrow I had longed for him to feel. The co-dependent part of my personality needed to know that my pleas to John had not fallen on deaf ears. I was so powerful that I could *make* him see the many mistakes he had made. *Once again,* I thought at the time, *I will step in and rescue him, and others will see what a good woman I am because I am able to change this man.* My own control issues played a big part in this. It wasn't all John.

Can batterers cover up what they really are? For periods of time, yes, they can. But they need a perfect life to do this, or when they face frustrations, the old habits will return.

Remember that domestic violence is about control. Batterers cannot ever be totally happy because their control knows no limits. It becomes more and more demanding, and soon it becomes a game to see just how much they can get away with before the victim finally leaves.

Foolishly, I believed that John had learned my limits and would never try to control me again.

My girlfriend always reminds me of something that is very true: "You can take a big pile of garbage and wrap it in beautiful paper and top it with a pretty bow. But when you open it, it is still garbage."

Our masks or wrapping often hide what we really are. John was gorgeous on the outside, but inside, he was still garbage!

I didn't think that Derek would want to go to the lake with John although he loved to fish. I was surprised when he accepted the invitation and even more surprised when his father agreed to it. My former husband had remarried, and his new wife had a son, Derek's age. Derek asked if Billy could come along, too.

John said, "The more, the merrier." Derek asked me to please bring Oreo, the dog, because he missed her.

But even before the planned outing, there were warning signals as plain and evident as the nose on my face. Once again, I chose to ignore them.

While planning our lake trip, John began making demands. He decided that since he was taking us and we were using his boat, I was obligated to sleep with him, in his bed, on the boat. This meant that he expected sex in return for his favors.

I immediately said, "No!"

Returning to his controlling ways, he said, "Fine. The trip is off! If you can't give a little, you can forget the trip!"

I calmly replied, "Okay, consider it cancelled." I knew he would back down—that he was just testing me. But why didn't I recognize what I was doing?

Maybe I did, but perversely, I just refused to stay healthy. Why did I continue with this charade? Because I wanted to. I felt I had the upper hand and was enjoying holding it over John's head for a change. I was playing a very dangerous game.

Of course, as predicted, John apologized and backed down. I lied when I told myself I was my own boss and wasn't going to allow any man to make demands on me. I was a vessel, full of empty words. There was no foundation to back up my bold statements.

Never truly admitting just how sick John was, the four of us (five, counting Oreo) set off on our trip. I can honestly say I should have, at that point, had my parental rights taken away from me. What kind of mother would put her son in harm's way? There was no excuse. I had, beyond a doubt, seen proof that this man we were now cruising down the highway with was crazy.

Looking back, there had been an event while I was living with John that should have convinced me that he was much sicker than any of us imagined. He had bought me a diamond-and-sapphire ring for my birthday. He must have purchased it sometime before and kept it hidden somewhere in the house. That day, we had been having a really bad argument. He ran out of the room and returned with a small black jeweler's box, which held the ring.

"What am I supposed to do with this ring I bought you for your birthday?"

He didn't know how to sit down and talk over problems. To him, an argument meant the marriage is over—that's it!

He pulled the ring out of its case and flung it against the fireplace. He then ran out of the room again, this time returning with a diamond tennis bracelet (I never said he was cheap!).

"I got this for you as a Christmas present. What do I do with it now?" He threw the bracelet in my lap.

Once he calmed down, I handed him the bracelet and picked the ring up off the floor. He had thrown it with so much force that it was bent. I put it back in its case and gave it to John. He then returned the gifts to their hiding place, without saying another word.

Later, on my birthday (the same day my mother had placed her "heartwarming" call), John proudly gave me the gift-wrapped box that contained the ring. He stood by me with a big smile, anxiously waiting to see my reaction.

This was no act. I tried to appear surprised while searching his face for some clue. When he tried to put the ring on my finger and it didn't fit because it was bent, he grew very upset.

"I can't believe this! They sold me a ring that's bent." He returned to the jeweler and made them repair it. I wonder what they thought.

As I'm sure you've figured out by now, he gave me the bracelet at Christmas and was excited about surprising me. Clearly, this was a man who not only behaved erratically and without remorse, but who was also capable of wiping his actions completely from his mind.

So what was I doing in a car with this man? Denying. Pretending. Forgetting. Returning to the familiar.

Maybe my father was right—I did need to have my head examined.

CHAPTER 12

The Reality Check

What can I say? It felt good to reminisce with John. It wasn't like being on a date, trying to get to know somebody. I had a history with him (albeit a short one), and we caught up on gossip about mutual friends.

I remember that a Michael Bolton tape was playing in his car. John played one of the songs and said it reminded him of me. I don't remember the name of the song, but it should have been titled "Gullible Woman."

John was going out of his way to be nice to Derek and Billy. They sat in the back seat and tormented Oreo and vice versa. The dog was as wild as ever, never running out of energy.

The boys were very excited as the boat was towed from dry dock and put in the water. It really was impressive. It slept six, and had a small galley and a bathroom with a shower. It made you feel as though you were somewhat special to be boarding this sexy vessel—one of those "eat your heart out" ego trips we sometimes go on. But if those envious people who were watching us launch this beautiful boat had any idea what we were about to go through, they would have thanked God to be standing on shore.

We followed a routine upon arriving at the lake. We sailed out quite far from the main marina, usually 30 miles or more; found a nice, large sandy beach that had no other campers or boats around; pulled the boat up on the beach; and set up camp on land.

Normally, the beach was used for lawn chairs, rafts, or campfires. We ate and slept on the boat. Since I was not going to be sleeping with John, we put sleeping bags on the beach. I could tell that this created discomfort for John. I'm sure he was convinced that, once there, I would change my mind and share his bed.

That evening, we sat around the campfire and talked about going fishing and skiing first thing in the morning. John fixed himself a drink, but I refrained. I didn't want alcohol to affect my judgment or lower my resolve to not sleep with him. I had made some stupid decisions before when drinking.

Although everything seemed to be going smoothly, I could feel John's tension. I knew it was caused by my insistence on sleeping with the boys on the beach. But he was going to prove himself on this trip, so he didn't act mean or pushy.

I knew the signs, however. I had seen them many times. We were going into the tension-building part of the domestic violence cycle. Accordingly, I played my part. I started joking and laughing, acting like a young girl again to cover the tension.

I remember a few things about this trip that were fun: the boys playing on rafts in the water of the cove; putting Oreo on the raft, which she loved; the boys trying to sunbathe on the sand with the dog running back and forth, jumping over their heads.

When Oreo's efforts didn't get their attention, she started

biting at their hair as she jumped over them. They finally dug a hole in the sand and buried her up to her head. Then, they ran back and forth, jumping over her head. She tried to bite them as they flew over her. She never did get tired!

One of the most enjoyable things we did was to take the boat out early each morning to a deserted spot by the high cliffs that overhung the lake. This not only offered shade, but was also incredibly beautiful. The water would look like a mirror—calm, and reflecting the cliffs.

The boys threw in their fishing lines and drank pop or Virgin Bloody Marys. John would cook a breakfast of bacon, scrambled eggs, fried potatoes, and toast. Food always tasted better on the lake. We would turn on the tape deck and play classical music or rock and roll—spending the day sitting on the back of the boat, enjoying good food, great scenery, and music.

However, one morning, what had normally been fun was turning into a disaster. John had woken up that morning in a bad mood. Lack of sex and not getting his way, I figured. I tried to ignore him, but it was getting on my nerves. Since the fish were not biting and I didn't want to be in confined quarters with him, I suggested we go back to the beach. He angrily started the boat's engines.

Just like I could read John's moods, he could read my fears. He knew I wanted Derek to have a great time and that I wanted to appear normal in front of Billy. I would try to tolerate his nastiness and be nicer to him so he would act decent. He had threatened me many times when we were in public to keep me under his control, "If you don't do what I tell you, I'm going to create a big scene and embarrass you."

Without actually voicing those words, he was threatening to do the same thing now. I had learned his patterns, and he was used to me falling into line.

John sat on the back of the boat by himself. Oreo, the boys, and I sat on the beach and played in the water. Derek asked me what was wrong with John. No longer willing to cover or lie, I said, "Just ignore him. He pouts when he doesn't get his way." My answer seemed to satisfy Derek because he didn't ask any more questions.

A large houseboat filled with adults pulled into the bay across from us. The boys watched as the strangers got on their jet skis and started riding them around the bay.

"Can we rent one of those someday, Mom?" I told Derek yes. He had always wanted to ride on one. Little did I know that he was going to get his wish fulfilled before the day was finished.

"Hey, Mom! Feed us! We're starved!" It hadn't been that long since breakfast, but they were growing boys. I hopped up to the boat and told John I was going to fix the boys some lunch. Was he hungry? He wouldn't answer.

I ignored him, and with a shrug of my shoulders, went below to the galley. I took lunch to the boys, and naturally they wanted seconds. Grumbling about a woman's work never being done, I jumped back on the boat and entered the galley, this time ignoring John completely. Screw him.

As I prepared the sandwiches, John's shadow covered the doorway. My heart began to pound, but I didn't look up.

"You bitch. I hate you."

I was not going to push him, and I was not going to argue with him. I was going to talk like I was having a normal conversation. "Oh, really? Why is that?"

"Because you are a ____." That name again. He wanted a reaction.

I continued making the sandwiches. "I'm sorry you feel that way, John. That isn't the way I feel about myself."

This conversation was going nowhere fast.

He continued. "It isn't important what you feel. What is

important is what I say. Your opinion doesn't count and it never has." As far as John was concerned, he was speaking the truth.

I wasn't going to continue talking to this stupid idiot! "John, why don't you do all of us a favor and go smoke a joint!" I had finished making the sandwiches, and even if I hadn't, I was getting away from him. I tried to push past him.

"You think I won't? I don't care what those brats think." He slid open the compartment where he kept his "stash."

I stood in the galley with the boys' food in my hands, watching and waiting. Suddenly, I realized that I didn't care what other people thought. If he wanted to smoke pot in front of the boys, how did that affect me other than showing my stupidity for being with him?

John must have realized I wasn't going to stop him. He had to either light up his stupid joint or shut up. Feeling backed into a corner, he did what he always resorted to. He lunged at me.

Food went flying across the kitchen. How do you struggle and remain quiet? My son was not far away. He would panic!

John threw me on the bed. He grabbed my crotch and began to twist and pinch. With my free arm, I hit him in the face. It didn't faze him. He put one hand on my throat and choked me and then started tearing at his swimming trunks.

Oh, dear God. He was going to rape me—with my son only a few feet away! I should have felt fear, but anger took its place. I remember thinking, *You son of a bitch. I'll kill you!*

Because he was somewhat distracted, trying to pull off his trunks, I managed to turn my head and bite his wrist so hard I thought my teeth would fall out! He drew his arm back and made a fist, preparing to hit me.

Taking a deep breath, I screamed at the top of my lungs, "Derek, help me!"

Did I come to my senses and realize that I had to stop covering up and resign myself to the fact that the truth could no longer be hidden? I had sworn to never drag my son into my dramas, but hadn't I forced the issue by taking him on this trip? Did I really, truly believe that John would change?

I think I hoped he would. Being as controlling as John, I was trying to force him to change. I was going to make him prove himself on this boating trip by taking Derek and Billy along. I foolishly thought he would never do something in front of two young boys.

I immediately heard Derek's bare feet hit the top deck. He ran toward the galley opening. John jumped up and tried to appear innocent. He looked at Derek as he entered the galley. Putting his hands in the air, he said, "I don't know what's wrong with your mother. She started freaking out on me and screaming."

Derek pushed past John and came to me. Then, my young, small 12-year-old turned to this six-foot-five man and pointed his finger at him.

"You leave my mom alone and go sit on the back of the boat!" Always my little hero. He should never have been put in this situation. John obediently walked to the back of the boat and sat down.

"Let's get our stuff off this boat right now, Mom."

We started gathering clothing and overnight bags and shoving them out the top front hatch. Derek made me leave the boat first, going last to protect me from John.

The three of us sat on the beach trying to decide what we should do. We were a long way from the marina. None of us had any great solutions. After an hour or more, John called to us. "Bring your things back on board. I'll take you back to the marina."

The boys and I stared at each other. "What do you guys think?" None of us wanted to get on the boat with this nut case.

Derek said, "I don't think he'll try and do anything with Billy and me along. We can sit at the back of the boat and watch him."

We decided, once safely back at the marina, that we would rent a car for the return trip home. We reluctantly climbed back on board.

Billy began handing our belongings to Derek through the hatch door. John sat at the back of the boat, not helping. I could feel his eyes burning a hole through my back. "You better stop acting so high and mighty or I'll tell your son what you're really like." Once again, threats to keep me under control.

I was really angry. Billy was grabbing the last of our belongings, and Derek was making his way to me. I decided it was time to call John's bluff. "Oh, really? Well, here he is, John, so go ahead and tell him what I'm really like. Now is your chance."

Derek stood looking at John, who said, "Your mother likes to fuck two men at the same time."

We stood there, speechless. What kind of person would say something like that to a 12-year-old boy? Especially about his mother? Where, in his dark, sick mind, did he come up with this? Derek and I stood staring at John.

"Don't pay attention to him, Derek. He always says stupid things when he gets like this. Let's get our things off this boat." I understood how people could pick up a gun and kill another person. If I had owned a gun, I would have shot John.

Before I turned to walk toward the front hatch, I turned to John. "You're really a sick man."

He looked at me for a second before dropping his head. "I know it."

There it was. All the blame and accusations he had leveled at me for being the cause of the problems in our marriage! He knew all along, and probably had known for years, that he was sick.

John continued to sit on the back of the boat while the boys, the dog, and I sat on the beach. "What are we going to do, Mom?"

I had gotten us into this situation, and I had better figure out a way to get us out of it. I stared across the bay to the houseboat.

"Do you boys think we could safely swim to that houseboat? It's a good distance from us."

They thought they could do it, although I had doubts about my ability to swim that span of water. But I had to attempt it. My only other choice was to stay on shore where John could get me.

"Let's go for it, guys."

We jumped up and began wading into the water. My heart was pounding. I have a great fear of deep water, and parts of this lake were so deep they had not been able to be measured until devices were developed to use sonar equipment.

I was about to swim into one of my greatest fears. The boys, being young and athletic, were way ahead of me, swimming like champs.

John saw what we were attempting to do. He started yelling at us to come back to the boat, that he would take us to the marina. He told the boys it was too far; they would never make it. I'm sure he feared what would happen to him if one of us drowned trying to escape him. We ignored him, continuing to swim.

It might have been because I was so emotionally drained or my fear of the deep water, but I soon realized I wasn't going to make it. My lungs burned, and I could barely lift my arms out of the water. I tried to dog paddle or float on my back to rest, but I was so exhausted I couldn't slow my breathing down. I could hear the water slapping up against my ears, my labored breathing, and my pounding heart.

So this is what it's like to drown. I was too tired to be scared, too cramped to fight it. Now I understood how people would just allow their bodies to sink down in the water. A peaceful feeling of surrender came over me.

My life began to flash through my mind, and I thought of how I had basically thrown it away. God had given me so many useful talents and I had not used them. I had just been gliding through life, not really caring about anything.

I had no important goals or missions. I simply existed and wasted time, waiting for old age and death. I had taken a useful body and mind and spent it to control others, criticize my fellow human beings, and live selfishly.

I had thoughts of what I could have done with my life lessons, how (if I'd gotten well) I might have helped other women who lived with batterers. I made a decision that I was going to live—and live so well that I would never be in this position again. I would use my knowledge and experience to help others.

I saw the boys far ahead of me, swimming and waving their arms at the people on the houseboat. At that moment, my foot hit an object in the water. It was a reef. I was able to stand on the tip of my toes and rest!

I gasped for air and thanked God. I watched as two men from the houseboat dropped a small dinghy from the back of their boat. Starting its small motor, they raced to the boys. After pulling them on board, the boys pointed to me, and they raced toward me. It was almost impossible to drag myself into the dinghy. But we were safe.

John began pulling up the anchor and untying his boat. He slowly pulled out of the bay. I believe he was expecting us to flag him down and ride in with him to the marina. We stood on the houseboat and watched him leave.

These kind strangers didn't ask too many questions. The

boys may have told them what happened when they picked them up. I was humiliated, but I didn't care. We were away from John and out of harm's way.

We called the park ranger from the houseboat's radio. Then, while we waited, our rescuers let the boys ride the jet skis. When I realized that our dog, Oreo, was still patiently waiting at the deserted camp, I sent the boys over to rescue her.

We boarded the park ranger's boat an hour later. I asked him about pressing charges against John, but he explained that where the assault had taken place was actually in a different state from the marina, where we were headed.

I decided it wasn't worth the effort. I wanted to be rid of him, not face him in court at a later date and drag the boys there to testify. We rented a car and headed home.

CHAPTER 13

Letting Go

I made an appointment with a divorce attorney. No more false beliefs and no more games. I was angry, but I was also scared. Scared by what I had done, scared by what I had put those sweet boys through, and scared that I'd never get well. I had proven that I was a long way from being stable.

I had taken the afternoon off from work to go to the attorney's office, which was located downtown. I very rarely ventured to this part of the city.

I filled out all the paperwork required by my lawyer. He was a man in his 30s with pictures of his wife and child on his desk. Looking at the family photos, I felt dirty—like a low-life. I still carried a heavy burden of shame.

I asked if I would be able to get an annulment since the marriage hadn't been especially long in duration. He said it was next to impossible to do and talked me out of trying. I agreed and left his office, but when I approached the main street, instead of turning right and heading for home, I felt led by some force to take a left, heading deeper into the city.

Driving past the Capitol building and courthouses, I finally found a parking spot in front of the building with the sign "Superior Court Records." I checked in through security and found the archives department. I was going to finally check out my nightmare. I needed to know the truth so my dream would stop and I could have some final closure.

There were clerks behind a long counter, and forms were available to fill out for the information you needed. I filled out my form with John's full name and social security number and signed my name at the bottom.

The female clerk looked at my form and asked, "Why do you want this information?"

I decided to be truthful. "I married this man, and something is terribly wrong. I need the truth."

She didn't seem surprised and told me to have a seat and wait. She came back in 20 minutes. "Which case do you want?"

Which case? There were *cases*! My dream! "How many are there?"

"Four."

My throat was dry. With a cracking voice, on the verge of tears, I answered, "Could I please see all of them?"

She told me it would take a while since the cases were 20 years old. I told her I would wait, and found a seat in the reception area.

The waiting room was packed. I overheard one woman tell another woman that I was a process server. Go figure. A man sitting next to me kept talking to me even though I didn't answer him. I felt like screaming! Out of character, I turned to him and said, "Shut up!" I was an emotional wreck.

Forty-five minutes later, the clerk brought out microfilm and directed me to equipment at the side of the room for viewing the film. My stomach hurt, I was having diarrhea spasms, and my hands were shaking so much, I had trouble putting the film in the machine.

I sat in the chair for three hours, sick at heart, viewing John's past.

Crimes against women. A crime against an elementary school girl. The first charge against John had been dropped because the city prosecutor wanted to focus on the second crime, which was more serious. However, because he had been acquitted of the second, more serious crime, he never faced the charges on the first, which would have required much-needed psychiatric help. He had been caught, but not really.

A strong inner voice told me to make a copy of the top page of each arrest and trial. I could not confront John with what I had discovered because I feared for my safety. It appeared that none of his current friends knew of his past because no word had been mentioned to me, and no rumors had been repeated. But at the time of the trial, he had been working for a large company from which he ultimately retired, so I'm sure a lot of his peers knew about it. Maybe that was why he never associated with them.

I had difficulty carrying on conversations at work for several days. My daughter kept asking me what was wrong, but I couldn't tell her. I couldn't tell any other person. I felt as though I needed to take a shower in disinfectant. I made an appointment with my doctor to have an AIDS test. Luckily, it came back negative.

Bob had left several messages for me to call him. When I was finally able to talk, I made an appointment to see him. I was really afraid to tell him what a stupid thing I had done, going to the lake and endangering my son.

He had always been very patient with me, but not today. It was time to get down to business and quit fooling around. He sat across from me as usual, with his hands folded beneath his chin. If I could read his mind, I'm sure it would have said, "What do I do with this woman?"

I stared back. It seemed like a standoff.

"I have been trying to contact you for several days. Have you been out of town?" he asked me.

Oh boy, had I! I wasn't ready to tell him what I had done, so I played innocent. "Yes."

"Well, the reason I called was to tell you that John is no longer coming to me for therapy. He didn't show up for his last appointment and is not returning my phone calls."

He didn't know what had happened!

I just said, "Oh."

Bob continued. "Di, I can't really tell you what John and I talked about, but I can tell you that his problems are so deep that I would never get to the bottom of them. I don't believe he really knows why he does the things he does. I will tell you for your own safety, you have to stay away from him. He will kill you."

I realized that what Bob was saying was indeed the truth. Somehow, when you're a victim of a violent assault, you still tell yourself afterwards that it wasn't really that bad. It's our way of not facing the truth. But if a stranger had done to us what our abuser had done, we would have called the police and been scared to death. Somehow, though, when "he" does it, we just deny, deny, deny.

"Di, do you remember the ring and bracelet incident? He honestly didn't remember throwing the ring into the wall or showing you the bracelet. He could be what is known as a passion killer. He would kill you in one of his rages and not remember doing it."

I thought back to the times when John's eyes would change and my words wouldn't reach him or have any effect on him. Once again, my past was flashing before my eyes. Throwing me through the door and being knocked out. Coming back to consciousness, with John leaning over me, crying. He was confused, wasn't sure what had happened.

John saying strange things that he knew weren't true. He claimed I was the one who got him laid off (fired) from his job. He told me I was the easiest "lay" he had ever had, although I had held out for what seemed like ages in the sex department. Not little lies, but the exact opposite of the true events.

I read that choking a woman or grabbing her by the throat was a passion killer's way of murdering. That was what John had always done. If it wasn't my throat, it was my breasts or vagina.

Anger at women. *Rape is about anger, with sex as the weapon.*

I finally looked at Bob. He must have known what was happening, because he remained silent.

"Bob, I have to tell you something really dumb and dangerous that I did. . . ." Like a person with a bad stomachache and terrible nausea, I literally "threw up" my story. Torrents of words, shame, and emotion were lying on the table when I finished.

Bob didn't show any facial expressions to let me see what he was thinking. He just stared at me. Finally, after what seemed like an eternity, he asked, "Why did you do that?"

"Hell, I don't know! Give me a break! I have no family. I love my children, but I ran Derek off, and it seems to be one big contest with my parents as they try to turn my children against me. I just grew tired of having no family, I guess."

Bob never swore, but I guess he couldn't help himself at this point. "That is the biggest line of bullshit I have ever heard!"

His remark stopped me in my tracks. I sat and stared at the wall, with my arms defensively crossed in front of my chest.

"Now, tell me why you went on this trip with John."

"I guess I'm just stupid."

"No. You're not stupid!"

I was really straining to think of a reason. There was not going to be any self-pity allowed or excuses.

"Maybe I just felt lonely. I don't know, Bob. I can't figure myself out. I don't know why I did it."

He let out a long sigh. "Don't you see? You were returning to the familiar. I can't make you stop doing this to yourself. I can listen and guide, but I can't force. It is up to you and you alone."

Faced with truth and reality again on my drive home, thoughts kept running through my mind. *Own your own power. Make your own decisions, but make healthy ones, not the same old ones that got you into this mess. Get it through your head, Di, before John or some other man kills you. Remember your thoughts on the lake when you thought you were going to drown. Live up to them.*

Once I was home, I turned off my telephone and sat and thought. I didn't have to beat myself up about the boat trip. I could use it as the catalyst that once and for all made me stop my self-destructive behavior. Others had done it, and so could I.

I sat for hours examining myself and my motives, which was an extremely painful process, but necessary. I was such a game player. The biggest game I played was with my life. I was trying to keep John hooked, so to speak. If I could make him feel that I still cared, he wouldn't be with another woman. I didn't really want *him*; I just didn't want him to be free. Why? *Control.* There was that word again.

Why wasn't I able to let other people live their lives? I

always felt I had to have the answer to every problem or question. To not have answers was to appear vulnerable. But what was wrong with that? I had to appear strong no matter what the cost. Approval from others—I thrived on it—it was my substance, my manna from heaven.

I once again began to read with a vengeance. I read books on love, shame, addictions, anger, women-haters, control, and co-dependency. I no longer thought of other people and their problems when I read. I applied it to myself and underlined the especially familiar traits I possessed. I made appointments with Bob twice a week. I was finally focusing on the right thing—*me!*

CHAPTER 14

A Sordid Past

Stalking seems to have become one of America's favorite pastimes. I've met many women who can't seem to rid their life of their abuser. Laws have done very little to remedy the crime. Once again, the burden of proof falls on the victim. The stalker always knows the fine line between breaking the law and just pushing it.

Did John stalk me? He really didn't have a reason to. Until the lake disaster, I had kept in touch with him. Why stalk the willing? I had convinced *him* as well as myself that our marriage still had a chance. However, he did start calling me in a harassing manner.

"I found a picture that you left at my house of your kids when they were young. Do you want it?"

I said I did.

"Too bad." I could hear him tearing the picture into shreds. I would hang up to make him stop. Whenever he would run across an item I had left at his house, we would go through this exercise, which I had learned to ignore.

I don't know if being served with divorce papers set him off or if he was just vindictively acting out, as always. I had to tell myself that the picture was just a material item. I had my memories that he could never destroy.

My court date for the divorce finally arrived. John had not contested it, so I figured he would not show up in court. I was right. After all the hell I had been through, the court proceedings were over in ten minutes. I had taken the afternoon off from work because I was going to go home and try to work up a pity party. I felt I at least deserved that!

As I stepped onto the crowded elevator that was to take me to the lobby, I noticed a court clerk standing beside me with an armful of documents. On top of the documents was a red rubber stamp. It said "Death Penalty."

I gasped in shock. Of course, all the people on the elevator looked at the item I was staring at. We were all taken aback. How often do you see something like that? It put my divorce into perspective. There were a lot of things worse than another divorce. I felt I had rid myself of my own death penalty by getting out of my marriage. No pity party. I went back to work.

I was opening the store early one morning when the phone rang. It was John. He was up really early. He must have had a bad night to be so angry at this hour. I had heard rumors that he had a woman living with him, which didn't surprise me. He couldn't stand to be alone.

"I found your scrapbook of your children's baby pictures. Do you want it?"

Here we go again. I knew he was speaking the truth because I hadn't been able to find the old family album when I unpacked. I didn't want to answer. I knew what he was going to do. I reached across my desk and opened my briefcase. "Yes, I do want that album, John."

As before: "You should have taken it with you when you moved out of my house."

I knew the next sound I would hear would be him tearing it to pieces.

I quickly replied, "Before you destroy my album, John, I think there is something you should know." I read the charges, dates of the crimes he had been accused of committing, and trial dates. Silence.

His voice lowered to almost a whisper. Was the new woman in the house? Why else would he whisper? "How did you find out about this?" His greatest fear, I'm sure.

Thinking I'd be safer if he believed another person knew about the evidence, I told him I had hired a private detective to check him out while we were still married, and it had taken him a long time to gather the information.

I could hear him breathing. "It never happened. None of it! I was acquitted. My wife and best friend knew I didn't do it. They were with me that night."

I acted bored. "Whatever." I then questioned him about the first offense, which he had never appeared in court for.

"That was a set-up! All of it was a lie!"

I had played detective after I read the complaints against John. In the first crime, there was a name signed on the bottom, but it was a man's signature. Either John had committed the crime against a juvenile, or against a woman who wasn't able to sign the complaint.

Apparently, a man in a company truck had exposed himself to several young girls as they walked home from school. To me, this seemed awfully bold because he could so easily be identified.

I called information for a listing under the signed name, and although it had been 20 years, the same people had that number. I talked to a woman and questioned her about the incident. She was more than happy to tell me anything I wanted to know.

I didn't feel like listening to John's excuses. "John, I know exactly where it happened, when it happened, and how you were identified by that little girl at a later date."

"What? That never happened!"

I wondered for a moment if perhaps he was never told how he had been identified. The young girl had been smart enough to memorize the company name on the truck and the truck number. Because of the information the girl had given the police, they were able to set up a trap.

The young girl, along with her father and a police detective, sat in a restaurant at the opposite end of the room from the front door. John's supervisor asked him to go to lunch at that same restaurant that day. (The police had informed the supervisor of what they were doing.)

The moment John walked through the front door, the little girl identified him. His truck, his company, his truck number, and now she pointed him out the minute she saw him. There wasn't much question about his guilt.

I could tell that John was scared. He began sputtering. He continued to protest his innocence. I didn't feel the need to hold this over John's head. What good would it do him or me? I just wanted him to leave me alone and stop destroying my property.

"John, I have no desire to destroy you. You will do that all by yourself. What makes me angry is, you never told me any of this. How could you marry a woman and have something like this in your past and never tell her?"

"Because it didn't happen. I was innocent. I was set up." Always the victim.

I ignored his excuses. "I should have been given the opportunity to decide if I still wanted to marry you. You deliberately hid this from me." I needed a question answered, just for my own curiosity. "John, is this what made you hate women, or did it happen before that, in your childhood?"

He offered no more excuses or defenses. He quietly said, "I don't know."

I think he was being truthful. He didn't know. I believe that somewhere deep down inside his dark soul, he felt good about getting it out into the open.

"Okay, this is our deal, John. I don't want any more of my property destroyed. If you find something of mine, I don't want you to call me. You can either mail it to me or have one of your employees bring it to my store. If you tear my family album up and ruin it, I am going to tell every one of your dear friends what I've found out. If you destroy my children's baby pictures, I will ruin you!"

Once again, he was going to be the one in control. "If you do that, I will sue you for slander."

"You can't, John. Your past is part of Superior Court records. It is there to read for any person who wants to read it. You can't sue for the truth; that is not slander."

If he could have gotten his hands on me, he would have killed me. I had no doubt about that, but I no longer cared. My heart and soul had been held captive by his threats too long. If he wanted to kill me, he knew where I was! I wasn't going to hide or play dead any longer.

He reverted to his past. He called me "the name." I guess he felt it would intimidate me or at least get even with me in some way. I couldn't believe that it had hurt me so much at one time to be called this by him. He was repeating the same behavior, and he wanted the same response.

"I have pictures of you that I took while you were sunbathing in the nude on the boat. I'm going to mail them out to all of my friends and yours, too."

I guess this approach was supposed to strike fear in my heart. "Please do that, John. It might help me get more dates."

I was tired of wallowing in the mud with him. I had divorced him so I wouldn't have to do this any longer, and here I was, lowering myself to his level.

"Listen, John. I don't want to argue with you. If you don't return my photo album, I'm going to make copies of the front pages of your charges and trial and put them on the windshield of your customers' cars in the parking lot."

Finally, after all the arguments and fights we had been through, he relented. "Okay, I'm sorry. I'll have one of my bartenders bring the album to your store today. I won't damage it or anything else of yours I find at the house."

Could this possibly be the end? Finally?

He continued in his nice-guy voice. "Di, let's be friends. Let's not try to hurt one another any more."

I almost laughed. "There's a problem with that, John. I *like* my friends. I don't like *you*." I hung up the phone.

As promised, his bartender delivered my photo album to my store that afternoon, unharmed.

I still didn't trust John. I wasn't sure if he would try to find me alone and hurt me. I was scared at night, alone in my apartment. My lease was up, and my friend Roberta urged me to move in with her. John didn't know where she lived, so I felt I would be safe.

Just to be cautious, I filed a restraining order against John. I needed the paperwork just in case he tried to contact me again.

My sister, Gail (left), and me, dressed for our cousin's wedding, at the ages of seven and five, respectively.

This picture was taken during my senior year of high school. I'm the one in the back row waving, with my mouth open (as usual).

Publicity photo taken when I was 27 years old and busily pursuing a singing career.

One of the many magazine ads during my reign as Mrs. Arizona.

This picture was part of my modeling portfolio. Look at the cleavage! No wonder the photographer asked me for a date!

This picture was taken during a telethon to raise money for a children's hospital. I'd left John six months before, and the stress still shows on my face.

My wonderful husband, David, and me, moments after taking our wedding vows. This time I did it right!

The man who saved my life, Dr. Robert Mosby, graciously posing with me during our wedding reception.

David and me on vacation in London, with Big Ben in the background. The trip was a surprise gift for my 50th birthday.

CHAPTER 15

My Spirit Begins to Stir

I have a very dear friend named Wayne. To look at him, you might be intimidated at first glance. He stands more than six feet tall, but his hair stands up straight on the top, making him appear to be about seven feet tall. The rest of his hair reaches down to his waist. He dresses like a member of a rock band, which is appropriate, since that's what he does for a living. He's on the road most of the time, serving as the keyboard player for a famous rock-and-roll star. To look at his outward trappings, one would never guess what a gentle spirit lives inside.

Wayne suffered at the hands of an abusive father. When his parents divorced, he lived with his mother, who was the picture of health. At the age of 55, she swam, jogged, and ran in marathons. She was the positive force in his life.

One morning, his mother woke up with a severe headache. She was in too much pain to drive, so Wayne and his sister drove her to the doctor. By that afternoon, she could no longer speak. She was in a vegetative state by that evening. After many tests, and ruling out a stroke, the doctor discovered that Wayne's mother had an extremely rare brain disease. Only 200 cases had ever been reported. She was in a coma for seven months before death took her.

Instead of feeling sorry for himself, Wayne began to realize how short and precious life was. This gave him the belief and drive to push himself in his career and do what he felt his life mission was. This sweet, gentle creature who looked like a man who might do drugs or murder someone helped me find my life's purpose.

While taking a break from his tour, Wayne flew into town to visit me. I was at my store, doing paperwork in the back room. Of course, my employees who didn't know him stared. He was quite a sight!

I was so happy to see him. We caught up on past events although he was always reluctant to discuss his business. He always wanted to know how others were doing, not interested in bragging about himself. I had to beg to find out what famous people he had met.

As we sat in the back room, he glanced at the shelf above my desk. "So, Di, let's take a serious look at this shelf full of your belongings. Let's see, there's a bottle of aspirin, a bottle of Stress-Tabs, a bottle of Maalox, and Pepto-Bismol."

I started laughing. I had never looked at it that way. I survived on these medicines every day. I should have bought stock in the companies.

He continued to question me in his calm but serious way. "Where's the Prozac?"

I couldn't fool him, so I sheepishly answered, "At my house."

Wayne had a way of making me question myself without getting defensive. He had learned so much through his own trials and sincerely wanted to help others.

"Di, something tells me you're not fulfilling your life's mission in this store."

He was right. The store was driving me crazy. My moods

reflected whether business was good or not. I looked at the weather through a retailer's eyes. Would it hurt business? Our state needed rain, but I hated it. People didn't want to come out in the rain. My entire life revolved around the store.

The worst part was my father. He had lent me the money to buy the business, and my payments to him were astronomical. Even when business was slow, he refused to lower the payments.

When I asked him if I could change the date of my monthly payment to him to the middle of the month instead of the first, he refused. My rent, royalty, and state taxes were all due in the first part of the month. When payroll happened to also hit on that date, it wiped me out financially.

The stress was making me wake up in the middle of the night in a cold sweat.

"Wayne, I can't sell the store. How would I survive?" I found it hard to imagine working for another person after being my own boss.

He calmly explained, "If you are doing your life's work, your survival will be a given. You have to stop looking at everything in life as a material possession."

Wayne was living proof of what he was telling me. "All the signs point to the fact that you were not meant to own this store. It's killing you." He was right. I sat and listened. "What would your life be without your father telling you what to do? What would happen to you if he were no longer in that position? Does that thought scare you?" he asked me.

Although I felt like I had cut the cord with my parents, I really had not. I was still under their control. My father had set up our business deal so that he could foreclose at any time for any reason. Had my father really done me a favor? Sure, he helped set me up in business, but actually he had set me up for failure.

Wayne continued to probe. "Di, do you think you've allowed yourself to be set up so that, once again, you are in a position to have your father lead your life?"

How true! Unknowingly (or maybe, knowingly) I had given my power away. What had started out to be a kind act on my father's part had turned into phone calls from him demanding things and accusing me of stealing from my own store.

Every time the phone rang, I cringed. I literally started shaking when he called. He ruined many days for me.

"Wayne, how do I find my life's mission?" I was more than ready.

He grew excited that I was finally listening. "First, you have to understand that God gave you talents, and I'm sure none of them include owning this store. What would you do, even if you were not paid for it, that would make you feel happy and fulfilled as a human being?"

Interesting question. Just what would that be?

"Second, all you have to do is ask God, your Higher Power, whatever you call it. There are many answers waiting for us. It means not only asking, but really listening to the answer."

As it did when I had sessions with Bob, my mind was exploring different ideas as Wayne and I continued to talk. Maybe I had actually set myself up to be a victim when I agreed to go into business with my father. I knew how he liked to control, and how we had always argued and had never gotten along. Still, I had closed my eyes to the known warning signs and jumped in head first, expecting to land on my feet. It couldn't and wouldn't turn out to be a success.

We continued to visit for an hour or so, and as he had done many times before, Wayne left town after creating a new awareness in me. What a wonderful friend to have!

With my new determination to find my purpose in life,

I started a new ritual. Each morning after completing all the opening chores at the store, I would sit at my desk and pray. I asked God what my mission in life was. I asked for divine guidance, knowledge, and wisdom. I was truly tired of running in circles and trying to be what others thought I should be.

I wanted, with all my heart, to live the life I was meant to live. I think my sincerity finally showed through. Even as I prayed, the wheels were starting to turn.

I have met so many beautiful women, inside as well as out, who have obvious talents. They say they don't know what to do with their lives. They are in a rut (remember, that's a grave with both ends kicked out) and seem to suffer from boredom and low self-esteem. They cannot see what is obvious to others. There seems to be a wall surrounding them that keeps them from moving in any direction. An object needs to be moving to be directed. I was no different from them.

I continued to work long hours but still prayed each morning, with the knowledge that my answer was on its way.

I guess I was shocked but not really surprised to hear that John had gotten married again. I heard through the local gossip line that the woman had been a bartender at a local restaurant and had two young children. I hoped that John didn't cause her children the harm he had put Derek through.

I had made up my mind to sell my store. I just hadn't worked up the nerve yet. I was still apprehensive about supporting myself, although I had done it before I had the store.

I didn't know what I wanted to do. I was really scared. I began to pay off all my bills and tried to save money—no easy chore for me!

I had started dating again, but I seemed to have a pattern when it came to men. I was no longer attracted to abusive men, but I was in my 40s and had no desire to date men younger than I was. Men my age tried to father me or control my actions. I met some nice gentlemen, but they wanted to "take me away" from this life I led.

"You work too hard for such a pretty woman."

What? Only ugly women work hard? They wanted to rescue me. I didn't want to be rescued.

Some of them wanted to take me on romantic trips. That appeared to be a fun thing to do, but that meant I would be expected to sleep with them. I wasn't willing to do it. I could no longer just give a part of myself away. It was a waste of my time and theirs, and it damaged my soul.

Other men thought that because I owned my own business, I must be rich. I could always tell, because when I would mention that I was thinking of selling my store, they would sort of panic. They saw what could have been a possible meal ticket escaping.

Some would try to find out my net worth by asking me questions about the franchise I owned. How much did it cost? What did you have to show as financial background to buy a franchise? Really revealing questions. Still others wanted to pick my brain about being in business for myself—sort of a short class in management.

But there were nice men. I dated doctors, private investigators, automobile dealers, insurance salesmen, actors, musicians, consultants, bankers, chefs, and one unemployed man.

One evening, I was having dinner with a nice guy. He had even put a small bottle of perfume on the table for me. As we sat and talked, I looked at him and thought, *Gads, this guy looks older than my father!* It was at that moment that I decided to stay home. I was tired of meeting new men. Actually, I was just plain tired.

I told Bob that I was bad dating material. I put men under a microscope and could pick out flaws in a flash. I had become extremely picky.

"That's good," he responded. "It's a sign of health and well-being. You should have done that a long time ago."

There was nothing wrong with being careful. I had been burned pretty badly, after all.

CHAPTER 16

Moving Toward My Mission

A year had quickly passed. Although I was still delaying, I had grown by giant steps in my journey to break free of old habits. One of my fears was contacting my father about selling the store. We hardly spoke to one another. If he chose to, he could refuse to allow me to sell. Then what? I suppose I was just putting off having to talk to him. Having conversations with him was one of my least favorite occurrences.

I had another significant dream. I lived in a large house. It was actually a nursing home, but I was living there. I heard a knock at the door and answered it to find my father standing there. No longer mean and harsh, he spoke to me kindly and said he was taking a trip with Mom. He had stopped by to say good-bye. He said he was ill and needed a vacation.

By this time, I had learned to pay attention to my dreams. I knew this dream meant that my father would be calling me, but not to criticize and tear me down as before. Something had changed. I started preparing myself for his call by praying and practicing my newfound ways. I was determined to be mature and calm.

He called a week later.

"Well, I have cancer," he told me. "I'm having surgery in three weeks. They're taking blood and saving it so I won't have to depend on a blood bank and possibly get infected blood." He had been diagnosed with prostate cancer, and he wanted to get everything between us straightened out before his surgery. I agreed that it should be done. The constant fighting between us had made me weary.

I used this time to tell him I wanted to sell the store. I agreed to wait until he had fully recovered from surgery. I was proud of myself. This was my first step toward freedom and independence. I slowly started cleaning out some of my personal belongings in the store. I had my employees go through the storage room and dispose of useless items. I was going to be prepared and not rush myself when the time came. I had a new hope and was losing some of my fear of the unknown.

I had been renting a storage unit, which held some of the larger items from the store that were no longer in use. I had agreed to donate them to the Jewish Community Center (JCC). There was only one problem. John had the key to the unit. I thought long and hard before calling him. After a month's time, I finally made the call.

I didn't want John to know I was thinking of selling the store. What went on in my life was none of his concern. I told him I wanted to clean out the unit and not have to make payments on it any longer. Like an old friend, he was very cordial. "I'll clean out the unit for you and bring the items to your house for you."

Why? What did he have up his sleeve? Why was he being so nice? He already knew I was thinking of selling the store. Then I learned that his newfound friend, my father, had told him. They had become best friends!

Since I now lived with Roberta, she could be there when

he delivered the items, and I wouldn't have to fear anything, so I agreed. I gave him the address.

On the planned evening, John showed up with everything in his truck. I helped him unload them and stack them in the corner of the garage to await the JCC, who would be picking them up. I couldn't believe my reaction when I was with him. Is this the man I was attracted to? I felt absolutely nothing, not even fear when I saw him.

After unloading the truck, John reached into the front of the truck and pulled out a six-pack of beer. He sat on the tailgate and opened a can. I guess he thought we were going to visit. He started talking about his bar and himself, never mentioning a new wife. He talked about the new house he had just built. It was almost 4,000 square feet. I started playing a little game, but not a harmful one this time.

"Gee, John. Isn't that an awfully large home for a bachelor?" I watched him squirm. "How many bedrooms does it have?"

"Four."

I wondered when he would break down and be truthful. Why was he pretending to still be unmarried? "Wow! Four bedrooms! What a huge house. Don't you get lost in it, living alone in such a big place?"

He couldn't look me in the eye. "No. You know me, always working. I spend more time at the bar than at home."

I began to smile. "Yeah, I know. I'm the same way. Work, work, work!" I was being borderline cruel at this point. I wanted to go for the kill. "How's business going, John?"

Time to brag. "Oh, really good. I can actually leave and go fishing with your dad once in a while. I showed a good net last month."

Which brought up a point. "That's great. Maybe you could pay me the $3,500 you owe me then, since business is so good." When he had first bought his bar, I had loaned him money to meet his first payroll. I would have done anything to keep him from losing his business and coming back to my store!

"Oh, uh, let me work on that. Could I make monthly payments to you? That is the only way I could arrange it right now."

I smiled. "Sure, I understand. Big house payments and all." It was time to put a stop to his charade. "So, John, does your wife know you're here, delivering things to me?"

He didn't bat an eye! "No."

"Where did you tell her you were going?"

He started to move around on the tailgate. "I told her I was helping a friend move some furniture."

"Did you tell her that 'friend' happened to be your ex-wife?"

"No."

I really wanted an answer to a burning question. "Did you tell your new wife about your past?"

He stared at the ground. "No. I didn't see the need to do that."

Just like he hadn't felt the need to tell me. "Are you telling me that you started off another marriage based on untruths and deception?"

He wouldn't answer. Actually, John didn't owe me any explanations. It was none of my business. I didn't really care if he had told this woman the truth. It didn't affect my life in any way.

"I did change some things. I built a new home so she wouldn't feel the way you had felt, living in a house where other women had been. I had our phone number changed to an unlisted one so old girlfriends can't call."

To John, these were great strides.

"Well, that's good, John. At least you tried some different approaches."

Just then, Roberta walked into the garage to tell me I had a phone call. When I returned, I told John I had to go to the store. He grabbed his remaining beers and left.

I had lied. I didn't need to go to the store. I just refused to continue to be a part of what John was doing—deceiving his wife. Why had he lied to her? If she had been uncomfortable with John seeing me, she could have come with him or told him to have one of his bartenders deliver the items. She could have also told him that it was my problem and I could take care of it myself.

I grabbed an iced tea and sat on the back patio, thinking. Hindsight. His old girlfriend losing her luggage while traveling and putting John's home address on the form she filled out so, when found, the luggage would be delivered to our home. Old girlfriends calling, but never when I was home. He would mention it in passing but tell me he had told them he was happily married. Finding pictures he had taken of old girlfriends in the nude, which he had saved and never thrown away. He had never really made a commitment to me, and now he was doing the same thing to his new wife.

By being somewhat nice to John, he felt I was ready to fall back into the trap. He was hoping to hide his new wife, or perhaps hoping to have an affair with me.

I found out later that John was beating his new bride, and she divorced him after seven months of marriage. Was he hoping to make me his victim once again? Who knows? Who cares?

Periodically, John would call me at the store to see how I was doing. I began to have my employees take messages, which I never responded to. I had been there, done that, and wasn't going to do it again.

CHAPTER 17

Getting Out of the Victim Role

The doctor said he believed he had gotten all of the cancer. He expected my father to fully recover and live a long life. Dad was heavily drugged and was cracking stupid jokes. My sister and I asked if they had a drug to make him funnier.

Dutifully, I sent flowers to my father's hospital room. When I wasn't working, I tried to visit him, but only when my mother wasn't there. She was refusing to speak to me—an old pattern that no longer intimidated me.

Dad would try to make me look at his incision, knowing I would probably pass out at the sight of it. Things of that nature made me weak in the knees. I laughingly refused. But when he was no longer on painkillers, his nasty disposition returned. He was nice to my sister, but not to me. Of course, it had always been this way, so I had grown accustomed to it. The only problem was, I no longer needed it or fed off it.

Once again, though, I willingly let myself be put in the position of becoming a victim of sorts. As a result of my therapy, I could actually see it taking place, but not being 100 percent well yet, I allowed myself to enter into this familiar territory.

It started out as concern on my sister's part. She was in town to visit Dad during his stay in the hospital. She called me at the store one day and said, "I have to tell you that I'm worried. I just found out that Mom and Dad don't have any health insurance. If something major happened, they could be wiped out financially. Would you do me a favor? Could you try to talk to Dad and see if you can talk him into getting some kind of insurance?"

Now, as I look back on the situation, I should have told my sister that if she was so concerned, she should do it herself. But still the rescuer, I told her I would try.

The next time I visited him, I mentioned "my" concern. My father exploded. "The only reason you care is out of fear of losing your inheritance. Mind your own business."

I didn't want to be around his angry and demeaning remarks anymore. I guess since they had gotten all the cancer and he knew he wasn't going to die, he didn't care about his talk of forgiveness or getting along. It was to be the last time I saw him while he was hospitalized.

That evening I examined myself thoroughly. Why did I hang around and take his verbal abuse? Was I willing to do this the rest of my life? If I continued to have any kind of relationship with him, I could expect things to go as before. He was not going to change. Could I accept it? No. It hurt me too deeply and harmed my self-esteem. I had jumped into the situation at my sister's insistence because she was afraid to do it herself. I got the verbal abuse and she went home, guiltless.

I decided to back away once again from my parents. It was the only way to survive. I didn't have the need to call and explain. That would only say I still wanted to argue or patch things up. I no longer wanted to offer explanations. I was simply removing myself from a bad situation. I had to.

I contacted a business broker and listed the store. The broker could talk to my father about the business, note, and so on.

I was owed money and intended to collect it. I still needed to survive, and I had put a lot of money into the store. I wanted to regain something for all of my hard work. I would no longer punish myself and allow others to walk all over me just to gain their approval.

I still prayed daily for God to show me my mission. I was learning that I still had areas of my life that needed changing.

Bob, my therapist, asked me, "Do you know how to stop being a victim?" Obviously, I still didn't know the answer to that question and gave him a blank look.

"This is how you do it," he told me. "You *stop* being a victim!" In a nutshell, there was the answer to a lifelong problem. You make up your mind that you are tired of being in the victim mode, and you just stop doing it.

We don't have to be abused to be a victim. We might be the one who others contact to do their dirty work—the gophers, so to speak. They take on a project that requires a lot of footwork and know we will be willing to do it for them because we can't seem to say no.

Our fear of confrontation can also put us in the victim mode. Our friends can treat us rudely, cancelling plans at the last moment in favor of something better that's come up, and they understand that we won't express anger. We will simply accept their actions without a word of complaint. We will be there for the next event, smiles and all.

We may still be connected to our parents because they hold the family purse strings, even when we are in our middle-age years. We bend and comply, as they not only tell us how to live our lives, but how to raise our children as well. They know we aren't going to argue or break free because we need their financial help. We've grown used to that extra financial bonus they sometimes throw our way, and we allow them to interfere because of it. We remain the victim.

We allow a man whom we work with to make sexually degrading remarks to us because we are fearful of rocking the corporate boat. He has learned, through repeated efforts, that we are going to smile and treat his words as a joke. We will even change jobs to escape him, rather than face him head-on.

Our children become tyrants who rule our homes with their aggressive behavior and rebellion. We fear what might happen if we put our foot down and restrict their actions. We hold our breath, just waiting for the day when they are raised and out of the house.

We haven't learned that love and respect go hand-in-hand. When we remain the victim, or in the victim mode, we haven't set any boundaries for ourselves. We have no clear-cut or defined lines drawn in the sand that tell others we are not willing to allow them to tread on our self-respect. We may complain about the actions or words of others, but we do nothing to change them.

Sometimes, we will use game playing to get a response from those who don't treat us fairly. We grow silent, waiting for them to respond and ask what is wrong. We detach for a short period of time, waiting for the apology. We feel sorry for ourselves and cry, hoping they will feel bad when they see our tears. We write long letters, which are never delivered, explaining how we feel, the pain they have caused, and the results of their offenses. We never have a face-to-face confrontation, setting our boundaries in concrete. We believe these offenders are mind readers. How will they know and understand if we don't tell them?

When we've set our boundaries, we have to be careful not to use them as a ploy to get even. This only opens the door for more pain. If there is a person in our lives who continually hurts us, it's acceptable to simply walk away. If our explanation is only going to cause arguments and strife, we don't go down that pathway again. We find a new path. We may have grown accustomed to arguing with certain people, and this is just another reason to do it. If we know we're right, we don't offer previous offenses to explain our case. We use our legs and feet to leave.

This is about changing. Change is something we are very fearful of. Why else would we remain with an abuser? Our victimization is deeply rooted. It is also a part of us that we have grown familiar with. But it isn't comfortable, and eventually we will understand that familiarity and comfort can be two very different things.

I was familiar with my father's verbal abuse—so familiar that it made me feel strange during those brief periods when he was actually nice. It was a side of him that was rarely seen by me, and I didn't know how to deal with it. If he had always been kind and soft-spoken, his rages would have frightened me. But it was the raging I had grown familiar with, so the periodic affability was not comfortable.

We have to examine when the familiar is no longer comfortable or not something we want in our lives. We need to look at the value of it and what it brings to us. Is it something that reaffirms our belief that we are undeserving of kindness or respect? Is it something that keeps us in the victim role? Is it something that keeps us from having to make a change? Does the familiarity harm our spirit?

I'm very comfortable with my current husband, David. We have a set pattern when he comes home from work. We talk about the day's events, his job, my writing, our children, and other things that may have taken place that day. If it's summer, we sit on our front patio, have a cocktail, and watch our horses grazing in the front pasture. I'm very comfortable with this routine. It makes me happy and content. If he came home angry and verbally abusive every single day, I would be familiar with it, but not comfortable. Do you see the difference?

We literally teach others how to treat us. We do this by accepting and conforming to their actions and behavior. Now they're familiar with our reactions. They've learned how far we will be pushed, what trigger words to use, and which buttons to push—all because we haven't demonstrated that it isn't acceptable.

Actually, defending ourselves can be somewhat intimidating at first. We may be tempted to back down and seek others' approval, after telling them we aren't going to tolerate their behavior anymore. We detest the feeling of not getting their acceptance, but after we've done it the first time and refuse to hedge on our commitment to change our victimization, we begin to sense a feeling of power. We discover that this new way of living really works! Then, our self-respect begins to turn to self-love. Along with these new emotions, we regain our power. It is something we will not ever lose again.

All of these new feelings will start to bring about change—and we learn that change can be good.

CHAPTER 18

Lies and Truths

What creates change? If something that we have been doing works for us, there is no reason to stop doing it. But what happens when something no longer works for us, or we decide we don't want to continue in the same pattern? Then we change.

At what point do you say, "I'm leaving—he's been beating me for years and it isn't going to stop"? When do you stop believing a lie? You stop when you learn the truth. And you learn the truth by no longer believing a lie.

I'm sure a lot of women will not be able to identify with me because they do not have the money to leave their abuser. "If I had the money, I'd be gone in a flash!" Please try to understand the point I'm making. I *had* the money, but I still stayed with John. Money was not the issue. A sickness or need inside of me kept me there. If I handed some women a fistful of money and told them to leave their abusers, they still wouldn't. The reasons we stay go much deeper than the pocketbook.

Since I ended my relationship with my abuser, God has continually placed battered women in my path. It might be at a luncheon or a meeting or at a tennis match. Once they find out what I do, they become an open book. They need to vent. They tell me what *he* has done to them. The conversation almost always goes something like this:

> *"I work [or don't work], and he handles all the money. I've been trying to think of a way to leave him, but he's home all day. I want to get all my possessions out of the house and I can't do it with him there."*
>
> *I reply, "If you work, why do you hand your paycheck over to him? Why don't you open your own checking account?"*
>
> *"Oh, I couldn't do that. He'd get angry and beat me!"*
>
> *Interesting. "But he's beating you anyway, so what's the difference?"*
>
> *"I just need time to plan."*
>
> *I ask, "How long have you been with him, and how long has he been abusing you?"*
>
> *"Fifteen years. He's been hitting me the entire time."*
>
> *"How much more time do you need to plan? You aren't planning; you're stalling. Just what is it you're getting out of this relationship that keeps you hanging on?"*
>
> *Silence.*

A prisoner wouldn't try to escape from jail without planning. It may take him two years, but at least he's been working on a plan. You cannot escape an unpleasant situation without thinking about it—not about ways to make it work, but ways to *leave*.

When we stop believing the lie that our abuser will change after years of hitting us, we are left with the truth. Why should he change? Is there a need? Hasn't he promised after every beating that it will never happen again? Why would it suddenly be different this time?

The lie: *He will change.*

The truth: *No, he won't. He doesn't want to. He doesn't need to.*

Our abuser only has our actions to go by. Our threats and words are empty. We prove that very fact each time we stay after a beating. *Your actions say that what he is doing to you is acceptable.*

I read a statement a long time ago that said, "Hit a woman once, and if she leaves, you've lost her forever. Hit a woman once, and if she stays, she's yours forever."

That calls for some thought, doesn't it? It's true! We tell our abuser, "If you ever hit me again, I will leave you, divorce you, take you to the cleaners, have you thrown in jail, etc."

He hits us again and we repeat our same threats, but we stay. Which do you think he believes—our actions or our words?

The lie: *We cause him to be angry and abusive.*

The truth: *His anger was there long before he met us.* It has absolutely nothing to do with our actions or us. He is angry because he wants to be angry. Remember that anger is a choice. He has chosen to be this way. But we've convinced ourselves that we're to blame. If we did things better or stopped making him angry, we wouldn't get hit.

The lie: *We want people to like our choice of spouse.* If we love him, we protect him. It might hurt his standing in the community.

The truth: *We take on all the shame.* We cover up the abuse so people won't think unkind thoughts about him. It is our own need to cover up and get the approval of others that keeps us silent. Our ego, pride, and low self-esteem come into play.

And, most important, if I let others know what's really going on in this facade we call a marriage, I will be expected to leave him. I'm scared. So, I pretend.

The lie: *I'm nothing without him.* I have no future without him.

The truth: *What kind of future are you talking about?* One that involves being beaten or called horrible names? That's a future?

What if we have never worked at a job? Usually our batterer wants us at home, isolated, so we have no job skills. What do we do?

Truthfully, you get assistance. I have not always had money. While seeking my first divorce and before child support had been court ordered, I started working at a local bank. I don't know how I kept that job. I knew nothing about banking. Going through the divorce kept me tied in knots, and I wasn't sleeping. I felt like a stupid, uneducated idiot on a daily basis. It was horrible. I would cry at night while lying in bed. I wanted to die.

I was not making enough money to support my children and myself. My about-to-be-ex gave me some financial help, but not enough to survive. It was his way of trying to force me to return to him. Of course, my father wouldn't help, so I did a little growing up. I applied for food stamps. It was humbling, but my children had food to eat. You simply do what you have to do! There is always a way out.

The lie: *I can't make it on my own.*

The truth: *Yes, you can.* Many other women have done it. Stop making excuses.

What if you're basically held captive in your own home? You're not allowed to work, you have no money, no car, and your spouse is beating you?

Guess what? There are shelters for women just like you. You can call them, talk with them, and if you feel you are truly in danger, they will arrange to meet you someplace and take you to a safe haven. Not only will you be safe, but they will help you plan your future, counsel you, and help you get financial assistance. It is an opportunity to start a new life. They will even go to court with you!

What if you have a job, a car, and your own money but are living with an abuser? Maybe he is just verbally or economically abusive. Perhaps he is a control freak. What then?

Guess what? There are support groups for women just like you, too! They usually meet once a week, and as you talk and share, you learn to regain your own power. I have seen women's lives changed by support groups. Sometimes, if a man is verbally abusive and discovers that his wife will no longer tolerate it, he changes. Sometimes.

Remember, a physical abuser, with counseling, has a cure rate of only 20 percent. That is with counseling. I never encourage a woman to stay with a man who hits her.

The lie: *I deserve to be beaten.* I'm useless.

The truth: *Nobody deserves to be beaten.*

When we are accustomed to men who treat us badly, it is all we know. It is all we expect. It is all we need. We have convinced ourselves that we are not worthy of a good man or respectful treatment. We have learned to survive on abuse. It becomes our "fix." We might as well just tell the guy on the first date, "I don't like myself. My father (mother) doesn't like me either. I know you won't like me because I am not likable. Go ahead and hit me. I need it, want it, and expect it. Thank you for fulfilling my prophecy of being worthless."

This is the truth. Before therapy, I could attend a party or business function and there might be 12 men at the event. Eleven of them would be kind, considerate, polite, and loving. I would somehow focus on the 12th man. The sick one.

Why is that? Because there was this self-loathing part of me that could find the man who also hated himself. Like tends to attract like—it's a law of the universe. It was my sickness reaching out and recognizing his sickness. We would inevitably gravitate toward each other.

The conversation in our minds was probably, "Hello, sociopath/abuser/misogynist/psycho. I need you to feed my sickness."

He would be saying, "Oh, hello, victim. I would be happy to oblige you."

Returning to the familiar.

Do you believe you deserve to be hit? Did your father hit you? If not, were you a pleaser as a child and never outgrew it? "Daddy's little girl." She knows that by being cute and coy, Daddy will approve of her.

Are you repeating this same behavior in your relationship with your abuser? Do you revert to a young girl's mannerisms when your abuser is angry? I did—with both my father and John. In the case of my father, this occurred in my adult years as well as during my childhood.

How do you feel after being hit, kicked, choked, or raped by your abuser? Do you feel intimidated, ashamed, submissive, or beaten down? Do you feel all those things? That is how he wants you to feel, and you have fallen into his trap. How convenient for him! Is it convenient for *you*? It must be. You stay.

Convenience—something to make our lives more simple. How simple and how convenient is it to live like a hostage? Once again, we have to get the lie out of the way in order to see the truth.

"You can't see the forest for the trees" brings about new meaning. How will you ever know or see the trees (truth) until you try something different? Just what is it you have to lose? You will continue to wander around in the forest, lost, never seeing the sunshine around the bend.

The lie: *All men are terrible.*

The truth: *Just the ones you have been attracted to.*

During a support group, one woman who was having a hard time giving up her abuser (although she was not married to him) stated: "These men are all the same. A bunch of creeps."

This wasn't true, and I had to speak up. "That is simply not the case. What is a fact is this: *You* are attracted to creeps. Likewise, you put out vibes, and the creeps are attracted to you. They pick up on your signals."

She was adamant. "No, they're all creeps. I'll never believe any differently."

I don't know why, but I started crying. I wanted to reach her. "Listen to me for a minute, please. Mr. Right could come along and knock on your front door, but you'll never know it because you'll be inside, in bed, with your abuser."

The lie: *No other man will be attracted to me.*

The truth: *Who told you that? Your abuser?* It is his fear surfacing.

"But I don't enjoy being hit."

Really? Then, why do you stay? Sure, it hurts. Who would enjoy it? You don't enjoy it, you *believe* you deserve it. Be honest. If you felt otherwise, would you stay with him? Of course not. The key to getting well is being honest with *you*.

It wasn't the beatings that made me leave John. It was the name-calling. What were my actions saying? It's okay to beat me, but don't call me names.

The lie: *I stay because I love him.*

The truth: *Look up the meaning of "love."* What you have isn't love. It is control (ours), fear, and obsession.

Because I love to write, I would pour out my emotions in long letters to John. I didn't mail these letters; I just wrote them. I had packed them away, but I ran across them later when I moved.

Yuck! They were full of self-pity and games. I could see just how controlling I had been. I was trying to make him feel bad for what he'd done. Then I'd tell him I couldn't live like that and never would again. Then I'd start asking him why he did the things he did. It was one big game, and it made me sick to read these letters. What was I thinking? I was trying to keep him hanging on through self-pity, denial, control, and immaturity.

Why do we deny? Because it is easier than changing. Let me give you an example. It is about a form of abuse, but not the physical kind. This is a complicated, sad story, but it makes a strong point.

I have a very dear friend named Susan who's a nurse. Her husband, Jim, is a doctor whom she put through medical school. They were married for 26 years and have two children. They lived in a beautiful home on the West Coast. Susan drove a new Jaguar and traveled to exotic places with her husband.

Jim was fun to be around, but he was very controlling. Susan resented this, but she would bend to meet his demands, complaining afterwards, but never changing. Then one day she called me and told me she suspected that Jim was having an affair.

I replied, "Why don't you have a private eye follow him and find out for certain?"

"I can't do that."

We both knew why. If she found out he was cheating on

her, she would have to either ignore it or confront him—which would probably lead to divorce.

In the end, Susan didn't have to confront Jim. After 26 years of marriage, he told her he was gay—not only gay, but also HIV-positive. He had a man on the side whom he was in love with and was moving in with his new lover.

Susan refused to believe it. I told her that even if she had an 8x10 glossy of him in the act with this guy, she'd deny it.

Jim moved out, and Susan was left alone. Her children were grown and gone. After one week, Jim asked if he could come home. He was miserable because his new lover stayed up all night and had friends over for parties. Susan agreed.

Jim and Susan made a pact. When he went from HIV to AIDS, she would help him commit suicide. He had worked with AIDS patients and knew how much they suffered. The couple also kept his disease a secret—nothing wrong with that except that he was performing surgery on a daily basis. It was a lawsuit waiting to happen.

Why did Susan help Jim live his lie? After 26 years of marriage, she was scared to be alone. Also, selfishness was part of the problem. Susan enjoyed the appearance of being a happily married woman. After so many years, how could she admit defeat? She had never been the type of person to care about material things. She just didn't want to start over at the age of 48.

Jim began to save vials of medicine for his upcoming suicide. Susan was tested for AIDS and was negative. For the first time, she was thankful that they had rarely been intimate. They were not going to tell a soul about this deep, painful secret.

Soon, Jim started staying out all night—seeing his lover, no doubt. Susan tried to cope but couldn't. She asked him to move out. They sold the beautiful home, divided property and money, and divorced.

Why would a woman stay with a man who was not only gay, but also verbally abusive and controlling? It's simple. It was easier than being alone. She was afraid to try something different. Susan would sometimes call me, crying, "How can I live on my own? I'll never make it without him."

But when we are living with an abuser, we really *are* on our own already. Is there emotional support? Is there comfort? Is there love and understanding? Only during the honeymoon phase after he has beaten the hell out of you!

Before you tell yourself that you would never stay with an HIV, gay, controlling man, you better ask yourself why you stay with a man who beats you. It's the same thing.

Susan denied Jim's double life. *You* deny your abuser's violence.

The lie: *By denying that I am abused, it isn't really happening.*

The truth: *Denial does not change the facts.*

Do you stay because deep down you enjoy feeling sorry for yourself? Come on, admit it. I had to! I sometimes enjoyed the newfound respect I received from John while wearing the bruises he gave me. It made him nicer. It was a very sick pattern.

You know the tricks of the trade—wearing short-sleeved blouses around the house so he can see the bruises. Wearing shorts so he can see the marks on your legs. Exaggerating a limp or movement so he will be sure to notice the pain he has inflicted.

It is nothing to be ashamed of. It is part of the pattern. What we are trying to do is make him feel the shame that he *should* feel. The only problem is, he won't feel it! If he did, he'd stop, so wise up! Who are you fooling anyway? You know the answer. Yourself!

The lie: *If I leave him for a short period of time, he will know I'm serious and stop hitting me.*

The truth: *Why would that make him change?* You still return to him. The abuser looks at our actions—that is, returning to him. This tells him we are willing to accept his abuse.

The lie: *My children need their father.*

The truth: *Get real! Do you understand what you're doing to your children?* You're destroying them! Stop making them the scapegoat. Although your children will be protective of you and hug you and cry with you after a violent scene, they will begin to resent you and lose respect for you. This is what happened to John.

Statistics prove that if you stay with an abuser, your son stands seven times the chance of growing up to become an abusive adult. Your daughter stands three times the chance of becoming a victim. You've taught them how to function in that role. *You* are their role model. Like your abuser, they learn from your actions, not your words.

Can you imagine being six years old and hiding in your bedroom while your father beats your mother? She's screaming and crying and begging for mercy. You hear him hitting her and kicking her and calling her names that a six-year-old should never hear.

What do you do if you're this child? You can't leave. You're a prisoner. You have no choices. You're forced to live like this. You don't want to bring friends to your house. Mom always has black eyes, or Dad might come home and start yelling. Then your secret is out. What a nightmare!

I believe that if domestic violence continues to grow in the numbers that it has, the courts are going to start removing children from these homes. Keeping them there is a form of child abuse. You may not hit your child, but there are things just as bad.

Your friends may be supportive, but let's face it—they're going to grow tired of listening to your sob stories. You ask advice but continue to live with the abuser. You don't really want advice—you want to vent.

Venting can do you good. The only problem is when you continue to do it over and over and over again. What good can that possibly do? It will not change your situation at home. Telling someone else what your abuser perpetrates upon you does not bring about healing. Talking about why you stay *will.*

The lie: *When he hits you, it is* your *issue.*

The truth: *Why he hits you is* his *issue—not yours.*

This is your issue—why do you stay? When you get to the bottom of your issue, you will start to get mentally healthy.

When I'm answering the Crisis Line at a shelter for battered women, I take calls from victims wanting to know if there are groups for men who batter. Their husband has not asked them to call. They do it on their own, to try and get him help.

The women are the ones who need help. They're trying to step in and rescue this man who doesn't feel the need to be rescued. They don't see the lie. If he really wanted to change, *he* would be calling and asking for help.

I have also seen women fall apart while staying at the shelter. After talking to their attorney and finding out that their abuser is going to fight back, they freak! One woman began sobbing after getting off the phone. "How could he do this to me?"

How could he do this to her? He had been beating her for 20 years, didn't care enough about her to seek help, and she's surprised that he isn't lying down and playing dead!

This is a very intimidating time. Because the victim has thrived on getting her abuser's approval, she is tempted to return to him. Any backbone she may have developed dissolves. If she becomes coy and submissive, he'll back off. She returns to a trap that has tightened even more.

Don't believe for one minute that the abuser isn't scared. He just knows how to conceal it, and he knows what buttons to push to make his victim back down. Controlling people feel the most fear when they lose their control. And statistics show that abusers become more violent when they sense that their victims may escape.

It is also terrifying for the victim to break free of an old habit, even one that is so damaging, so life threatening. I've seen women whose beauty has disappeared as a result of domestic violence. They might have a nose like a boxer (from being broken so many times), scars around the mouth from being punched, and dentures or bridges because they've had their teeth knocked out. The list goes on and on, yet they say they can't live without these men. But they won't continue to live much longer if they stay.

Who can call that *living* anyway? What kind of life is that? It sounds more like a slow death.

CHAPTER 19

Life after Abuse

I finally sold my store. I refused to take less than the asking price—I knew what it was worth. Since my father held the note on the business, he felt he had a say. I told him I refused to put myself in any kind of financial bind by taking less. I would have to live on the profits I made for some time, and I wasn't going to create stress for myself.

In character, he said, "What difference does it make? You had nothing before you had the store."

Isn't a father supposed to be concerned about his daughter's welfare? I refused to justify his cruel comment with a response. I had decided I would only talk to my father about business—never anything of a personal nature. When he'd start to attack me personally, I just said, "No, we aren't going to do that. I will discuss business with you, but nothing else." What could he say? Nothing.

But what I can say is: Thank you, Dr. Mosby, for helping me in that area!

The buyers finally agreed to the terms. Everything went as smooth as silk. I knew I had made the right decision and that God was helping me. I stayed to help train the new owners and show them all of the store procedures. Then I was free. No more daily stress, and most important, no more horrible phone conversations with my father. A new life was ahead of me.

My sister, Gail, divorced. My father gave her $60,000 to get on her feet—a gift, not a loan. When I heard this news, I wrote him a letter telling him how unfair he was and that I never wanted to talk to him again. Then I threw the letter in the trash. Why bother? Just like with John, did it really matter? Would it change my father? I was now 45 years old, and it had always been this way. Would it change? No, to all those questions. So I set about getting even.

Do you know how to get even? You lead a happy, carefree life filled with love and compassion. You do not allow those who would seek to destroy you into this new life. Not in your thoughts or motives. Inner peace is a powerful tool.

I will always remember a comment a friend of mine made that helped me, and I believe it will help you, too. I was buying an outfit for some social function, and two of my friends were with me. I couldn't decide which blouse to wear under the suit. One of my friends said, "I think you should wear the low-cut blouse and look sexy."

My other friend responded, "Oh, no, you should never wear clothes to try and look sexy. You let your sexiness show through in your face."

She wasn't talking about makeup. She was talking about the sexiness a woman has when she is self-assured and believes in herself. I'm telling you, a self-assured walk, a nice smile, eye contact, a firm handshake, and the knowledge that you are living your life to its full potential will bring a man to his knees!

The only men who do not like this kind of woman are those with low self-esteem who feel threatened by her, or the men who believe a woman should have no mind of her own. If you happen to meet either kind of man, run!

Six years have passed since I sold my store. The new owners are doing great and are very happy. The employees who worked for me still keep in touch and send me cards on Mother's Day. I love them.

I have paid for three of my four children to receive therapy. I can't go back and undo the harm I caused as a result of the way I lived my life and the way I tried to control them. I had repeated my parents' behavior and had acted like a dictator toward them, but what I can do is be a good mother now. I consider my children my closest friends. I don't tell them how to live their lives, but I *will* give advice when asked.

Admitting to the mistakes I had made with my kids brought about a healing in my daughters' lives. It took the pressure off them to know that I owned up to my responsibility. And I not only owned up to it—I apologized for it. It is never too late to ask for forgiveness and admit the error of your ways.

Derek is now a young adult attending college. When John's name is mentioned, he still gets angry. He would love to inflict pain upon him. Although I have stressed the need to move on and to try to realize how sick John is, I can understand how Derek feels. This man physically hurt his mother and made his young life miserable. I've tried to impart to him that holding on to anger and grudges only harms *us*, not the other person.

"Delight yourself in the Lord, and He will give you the desires of your heart." This does not mean being submissive to an abusive husband. It *does* mean knowing and experi-

encing your own desires—not another person's.

What were my desires? To be happily married to a kind, generous gentleman. Don't laugh at this: to live on a farm or ranch with horses, dogs, geese, and cats. To have a deep, close friendship with my children. To be in a financial position to help battered women.

I have realized all my desires! Why? Because I finally believed that I deserved them. Love and compassion have helped me overcome every negative thing that John or my father did to me. Because I got well myself, I was able to be attracted to, and attract, a healthy man. In the same respect, I began to attract healthy events and people into my life.

"As a man thinketh, so is he." My positive thoughts and beliefs in myself had turned my world and my life around. This was no mistake. I now work with battered women, and I also speak to groups to educate them about domestic violence. I have founded an organization whose mission it is to go into schools to talk to preteen and teenage girls. They need to know the signs before they get into a toxic relationship. *I am fulfilling my life's mission.*

Because I travel quite a bit, I've met a diverse and interesting group of people. I met two different psychics at separate social events who both said the same thing: "I see you talking to large groups of women, teaching them about something you learned in your own life." This blew me away! Psychics have always scared me, but this caught my attention.

One of them said, "You should be writing. I see you sitting at a computer, typing. This is very important and something you should do right away." That was years ago. Obviously, I didn't jump into it right away.

I located a local volunteer agency and told them that I wanted to work with battered women. They put me in touch with a shelter. I am now on the Advisory Council, plus I do whatever I can on the side. I will speak at the drop of a hat. I will talk to anyone about domestic violence who wants to discuss it.

God, for some reason, started giving me insight into the battered woman's mind. I had read a lot of books on the subject and learned through my therapy, but the insight I received came about as a result of going into my own mind and admitting why I had allowed myself to be battered. This required total honesty and no excuses. Why bother trying to fool myself? If I did that, I would never be able to really help another victim. You can't help a woman who has been beaten by stroking her hair or rubbing her shoulders while telling her how sorry you are. Of course you have to show compassion and hug her, but what I'm trying to say is, pity will not help her extricate herself from the situation—making her question her own motives *will*.

When a woman asks me a question, I go back to my own situation and remember how I felt and why I responded the way I did. There is no room for lies, but I do not feel shame for the way I felt or acted. I was sick. I am now well.

A friend or a woman I have met will ask me if I will talk to a friend who is being battered. Of course I will—in a New York minute! We meet somewhere or she comes to my house. I will listen for a while and ask questions and then gently cut the person off. I don't need to know all the horrible things he's done to her to get the picture. All of our lives are similar. The batterers all have the same traits. But when I begin to question the victim and try to make her responsible for her own actions and motives, her friend will almost always look at me with shock.

I'm sure I sometimes come across as insensitive, but I don't have much time to make a victim understand what's going on! It may very well be the last opportunity I have to talk with her. I have to get to the real issue, which is why she stays. I have to plant a seed that will hopefully grow and blossom. She needs to ask herself a lot of questions that have nothing to do with her abuser—only *her*. It is not a lack of sensitivity. It's trying to get to the truth by getting the lie out of the way.

The O.J. Simpson murder trial brought about a new awareness regarding domestic violence. A lot of people jumped on the bandwagon and began speaking out against it. We don't need to exaggerate how many women are beaten. Let me give you a few statistics:

- Over 50 percent of all women will experience physical violence in intimate relationships. For about 25 percent of them, the battering will be regular and ongoing.[3]

- Most prevalence-rate studies estimate that 28 percent of all adult women in a relationship are victims of domestic violence on an annual basis.[4]

- Almost four years ago, the Surgeon General of the United States warned that violence was the number-one public health risk to adult women in the United States. And, as of June 1992, it still remains the leading cause of injuries to women ages 15 to 44—more common than automobile accidents, mugging, and cancer deaths combined![5]

- Battering is the major cause of injury to women, resulting in about one million visits annually to physicians.[6]

I could fill many pages with statistics. It is obvious that we don't need to make the number of abused women any higher than it actually is. The facts speak loud and clear.

Imagine the changes that could be made in our society if more formerly battered women began to speak out about their own experiences and help others who are living the nightmare. One person, speaking from experience, can make a great impact. But if you've never been abused, all you can do is quote statistics.

We have to own up to our faults and mistakes. We can learn from them and move on. If we don't take this important step, we will remain emotionally tied to our abuser. We must not only leave physically, but emotionally as well.

Let's talk about recognition and how to heal.

PART III

The Healing Process

CHAPTER 20

His Warning Signs

Have you ever looked at a painting or drawing and wondered why the artist painted it? Paintings that are pastel in color, with beautiful flowers and trees and a peaceful stream or lovely landscape show the artist's appreciation for the beauty that surrounds her and the desire to share it with other people. However, when I see paintings that are black and red—depicting a poor lost soul in torment with a disfigured face and tears streaming down the cheeks—I cringe when I think about what that artist might be trying to express.

You need to do this same appraisal when meeting a man. You must really listen to his words and determine what he is trying to say. You can learn to read between the lines, but it takes time until you become proficient at it.

You may be required to become a scientist and put the man under a microscope. Don't just hear the words and accept them. What is he *really* saying? There are many clues he will unwittingly give you. Don't look for the obvious such as throwing temper tantrums or verbally abusing you. Don't believe for one minute that an abuser doesn't know how to play the game and pretend to be something he's not.

Remember, John never displayed any kind of wrathful behavior while we were dating. He knew I was watching him.

This also means no whirlwind courtship. Too many women rush into a relationship out of loneliness or fear. Especially in cases involving violent personalities, this can be a dangerous habit.

An abuser will not always expose his violence at the beginning of a relationship. His true personality and mode of behavior are often kept hidden until he feels it is "safe" to reveal himself. If you really want to see what's going on in his mind, then watch, listen, and observe very closely. If there are aspects of his behavior that alarm you, pay attention to those warnings. Our intuition tries to tell us things to protect us, and we need to learn to listen.

Do not, for any reason, tell yourself that you can change him. You *can't*—especially if the problem is violence related. The best way to predict whether you are involved with an abuser and aren't aware of it yet is to examine the following areas.

Inability to Control His Emotions

Listen to the man's stories. How did he handle certain situations in the past? Pay attention to his friends as they recount interactions that they've had with this man. I mean, really listen—not with your heart, but with your head. What do old girlfriends say about him? Don't be in a hurry to chalk up their negative remarks to jealousy or spite.

Does he have a history of violence? If he has been violent in the past, you can pretty well assume that he will be again.

Does he become enraged in response to minor incidents—those that most people would ignore? This is really a telling sign. If you marry this guy, look forward to constantly trying to settle him down, or turning into a "little girl" to try to calm him. I guarantee that this will produce headaches, stomach ulcers, and tension. Not in him—in *you*.

When he's angry, does he hit walls or some other object? This is a sure sign that he does not have control over his temper. It all starts with walls or doors. But trust me, someday he will be hitting your face. It is only a matter of time.

Do you have to avoid certain topics to keep the peace? I did with John. That was horrible! Here is an adult man, and I had to walk on eggshells not to antagonize him. Talk about control—I was like a trained dog. He was a big baby, getting his way.

And when you're out with another couple, do you sit there, tied in knots, waiting for the other shoe to drop? Are you afraid he may say or do something to embarrass you in front of them? Are you worried that something you do or say will cause you to be beaten up when you get home?

Inability to Maintain Good Relationships

Does he keep you away from his friends and family? If so, he's probably hiding something. He has no friends? There must be a good reason. Don't try and rescue this lonely soul. Even "loners" have at least one good friend.

If he's been married before or has previously had a long relationship with another woman, does he talk about it often, and does he appear to be resentful? If so, he has a lot of anger inside him and has not resolved these issues yet.

This brings up a good point: Try not to become involved or even date a man who has just come out of a marriage or long relationship. He doesn't need your help in "getting through" his sorrow (or anger). Divorce is a very emotional experience, and it takes time to work through these deep-seated feelings. You don't want to be a rebound victim.

Family Background

What is his family like? Do they appear to love and respect each other, or are they dysfunctional? Do they fight and scream? Are they heavy drinkers? Do they openly criticize their son, this man you're dating? Remember, whether we mean to or not, we emulate what we've seen our parents do.

Controlling Behavior

Are you allowed to express your opinions? Does he insist that you do everything together and get upset when you do things without him? Boring! You cannot have a full life without friends. This is a very strong signal to be cognizant of.

Is he so jealous that he wants to know every place you've been? This is not love. This is the beginning stage of control. Simply by being challenged by you and told it is none of his business will not put a stop to it. To gain your approval and get back into your good graces, he will apologize and attempt to behave himself for a period of time. But it never lasts. If you stay with him, you can expect to have all your rights taken away.

Does he play mind games with you? Does he test your love for him? This is the time to really listen to his words. When you're having a conversation with him, do you feel that you always have to explain yourself or your actions? Do you continually have to convince him that you really care about him?

People who need to be reassured all the time are very insecure. They do not usually outgrow this syndrome without counseling. You should not be required to "build them up" on a regular basis. If you feel that a man you're dating needs constant reassurance, run! It isn't going to get any better.

Problems with Authority

Does he seem to have problems at work? It can't always be the boss's or some co-worker's fault. He obviously has a problem with authority and other people. If nothing *you* ever do is right, then why would he think his co-workers might be justified in their actions?

Addictions

Does he seem to have a problem with drugs or alcohol? Once again, look at his family. Alcoholism is an inherited disease. Even though he may have hated the fact that one or both parents had a problem with it, there is a good chance he could be dealing with this same issue.

This isn't always the case, but keep your eyes open, especially where drugs are involved. Drugs mask self-hatred, and self-hatred creates anger.

Lack of Respect for Others

Is he a chauvinist? This is a popular word from the '70s, but it still applies today. If you're treated like an inferior individual or told that you should "know your place" and that the man is the boss, you're with a very domineering, controlling man.

I'm not saying that a couple in a relationship will always agree, but there must be a healthy compromise that doesn't offend either party. Together, they must reach a decision that is mutually acceptable and that won't create resentment in the future.

Self-Deception

"But he needs me." Does his neediness create an attraction? Remember that this is a sign of sickness. It is *very* unhealthy. A healthy relationship is based on more than a psychological dependency.

"But I can change him!" How often we women say that when faced with major problems in our relationships. Sometimes, as women, we're deaf. We don't listen to what a man is telling us. However, you learn to do so be being hyper-observant. I'll give you some examples.

Let's talk about a man named George. George is a successful senior vice president of a large company. He has been divorced for several years. He has a beautiful home and drives a nice car. He is friendly, athletic, and outgoing. He takes you on expensive and exciting dates. Listen to what he says, and then I'll tell you what the truth of the matter is.

He says, "I told my former wife that I was willing to go to counseling when she asked for a divorce."

He hadn't been willing to go while married and hadn't paid attention to their problems until they got out of control.

"I told my former wife that I knew I had insulted and embarrassed her in front of people and was trying to stop myself from yelling at her." *He is verbally abusive. You will be treated in the same way.*

"My secretary tells me I'm a good catch. She says there aren't many men around like me with a good job, great looks, and a nice home." *He wants you to agree with his secretary and reassure him that he has all those fine qualities.* Let his secretary date him!

"I think we would be really good in bed together. I like to do___, ___, and ___." *He wants to know if you find him sexually attractive. Usually, if a man has to tell you how good he is in bed, he can't live up to it in real life. He feels inadequate.*

"You dress so casually when we go out. I don't know if you would fit in to the corporate world." *This man is getting ready to groom you. Expect to be told what to wear and how to act. Tell him you aren't sure he fits into* your *world.*

Other Warning Signs

If a man buys clothing for you that is very revealing and expects you to wear it in public while you're with him, don't allow this to happen. He wants other men to look at you so he can feel superior when he's with you. You don't want to be a sexual pawn. You want to be respected in your own right—and not because you look like a streetwalker.

A recently divorced friend told me, "It's going to be scary to start dating again after so many years of being married. I know I'm vulnerable. How will I be able to get a read on a man and tell if he's decent?"

We aren't always able to get a "read" on a man, especially if he's adept at covering up. One thing that helped me was that, by learning what made *me* tick, I found it easier to see what ran other people's clocks.

When I hear a woman make a particular statement, I can think back to a time when I may have said the same thing and remember why I did it. I can also remember John doing it. Because my life was shame-based, I can immediately see this characteristic in another person. That's why it's so important to know your own patterns. It helps you see someone else's. But don't turn this around and try to see a physically abusive man's motives and make excuses for him. There is no excuse! Run, baby, run!

What about the verbally abusive man? Would you really want to waste your life living with a man who yells and screams? From what I experienced in my childhood, I can tell you that living in a home where this continually occurs is a nightmare. They say that words can't hurt, but I beg to differ. Long after bruises have healed, the words remain to haunt and damage you.

I look at pictures of myself from my childhood. When I was very young, I had this little cherub face and sparkling eyes. As I grew older, the emptiness and confusion showed in my face. Finally, in my teens, the anger really came out. It makes me want to cry.

Imagine a life waiting for the next explosion. What will set him off? You have to cover up your children's mistakes so he won't yell at them. You can't discuss certain topics at the dinner table or he'll upset everybody. You soon learn what buttons not to push and try to leave the house when you see that it might happen. You live your life with your stomach tied in knots: smiling and covering up, focusing on damage control, wringing your hands, getting physical problems. The list goes on and on.

These people literally make you sick. Why do you tolerate this behavior? Life wasn't meant to be lived that way. Why would you choose this over a happy, stress-free life? Were we called into this life to be miserable and suffer endless, needless pain? No!

Some people are simply toxic. They're filled with tons of

unresolved anger and don't care to get to the bottom of it. It has become a way of life, and they're happy to live like that. It gives them a thrill to tell other people off, insult and degrade them, write abusive letters, and so on. They're most excited right after "sticking it" to someone.

I don't see a lot of hope for these individuals. Unless they become so miserable that they see a need to change, they won't. You *must* walk away from them. Otherwise, their toxins will infiltrate themselves into your life. That is poison to your mental health.

I knew a woman who was as beautiful inside as she was outside. She was the first to bring food when someone was ill and would offer to run errands—a truly good person. The problem? Her husband of ten years talked abusively to her. He called her an "asshole, bitch," and worse. One day she asked, "Will I ever be happy, Di?"

I asked no questions. I just told her, "You are the only one who can determine that."

She began to cry. She told me the horrible things her husband said to her and how it made her feel. But still she stayed. Why? She was tied to him financially. They were living in her house, but he did not give her much money even though he had a very successful business and could afford it. She also feared he would start dating other women if she kicked him out. She had told me some of the sexual remarks he had made to other women. They were cruel and demeaning.

Our conversations over the course of a few months went like this:

> *"Do you believe you're all these names he calls you?" I would ask.*
>
> *"I am an asshole. I'm an idiot," she would reply.*

"No, you aren't. You are nothing like what he calls you."

"Well, I feel like it! Why else would I put up with it?"

"Did your father treat you cruelly?"

"Yes. He called me terrible names and even tried to sexually molest me."

"Don't you see? You're repeating a pattern!"

"But I can't leave! What if he starts to see other women?"

"Don't you think if he's making sexual remarks to other women right in front of you that that may already be a possibility?"

"Oh, I hate myself. How can he respect me when I don't even respect myself?"

Good point. How can we expect to be treated with respect and dignity when we so readily allow the exact opposite to happen? My friend and I talked often. I tried to make her see what was happening in her marriage. If she never told her husband that she abhorred his abuse and would not tolerate it, what impetus would he have to cease the behavior?

I started to notice that she would no longer talk to me about her situation. I knew what was happening. She didn't want to be in a position where she had to make a decision, so she chose to live with the abuse.

I told her, "You know, you don't have to leave your husband to change your life."

Her eyes lit up! This took away her greatest fears.

"I know a wonderful woman who is a counselor who deals with all forms of abuse. I think she'll be able to really help you," I told her. She made an appointment in a flash!

In a matter of months, after seeing the therapist on a weekly basis, this woman had changed immensely. So did her husband and their marriage. When her husband would call her names, she would forcefully state, "That is verbal abuse, and I will not take it!" He would stand with his mouth hanging open, sputtering.

He tested her. Arriving home one Friday evening after work, he said, "I think we should separate. I'm not happy." At one time this would have brought her to her knees, begging and pleading. But this time, she looked him straight in the eyes and said, "I think you're right! What would I be missing if you left? A man who calls me names, is never there when I need to talk, and can't even wrap his arms around me at night! I'm not leaving—this is my house. *You* get out!"

Bingo! He immediately apologized. Their marriage has completely turned around. After ten years, they have finally bonded. Her husband treats her with respect now, and when he slips into his old ways, she immediately calls him on it.

However, the above situation is one of the few instances where there was a happy ending. Usually, abuse will not cease just because one spouse gets therapy. A very controlling person will not give up the fight. If he can cause fear in you by being verbally abusive and it seems to be getting more severe, you'd better leave. It usually means that physical abuse is just around the corner.

Counseling can definitely help an abused person gain control over her life. But can it also help the abuser? For it to work, the abuser must first admit his wrongdoing. Do I believe batterers are sorry? No. Why don't they seek help if they are? Very rarely will a batterer own up to his abuse. He will blame the woman, or the pressures at his job. Mostly he denies that it happened at all. Some men are even able to convince their victim that it did not happen—that she's crazy. After repeated abuse, the victim becomes so confused, so unable to think clearly, that she actually starts to believe that perhaps *she* is going insane.

Does he have a criminal mind? Well, he *is* breaking the law when he hits his wife or girlfriend. You tell me.

I heard a speaker tell a funny joke at a luncheon. "How many psychiatrists does it take to change a light bulb?" Answer: "Just one, but only if the light bulb wants to change." It was funny, but very revealing. We don't change unless we want to. Abusers may go to therapy, but only after being forced into it by their wives. In those cases, I have never heard of positive, lasting results.

If a couple has sought joint counseling, the women all say the same thing: "I can't believe the way he acted—nice, mannerly, innocent, and falsely accused. He handed out one lie after the other."

If your spouse wants to seek counseling on his own and not after being forced into it by you, he should go to a different counselor from the one you are seeing. A therapist will never be able to get to the bottom of the abuser's problems with you sitting in on the same session. Also, it's important that the counselor be trained in dealing with domestic violence. Unfortunately, many ministers, rabbis, and priests do not understand the true nature of the problem.

When you're dealing with an abuser, you are working with a very sick, angry, and controlling mind. He is not "demon-possessed" (that is what my minister told me); he's not just a sinner who needs prayer and forgiveness; and you're not a woman who needs to be more submissive or obedient or who needs to pray, fast, or go to church more often. All the prayer in the world will not make him stop hitting you, and this is coming from a woman who believes in the power of prayer.

When I would speak with my minister and pray with him, only to go home and get beaten, it ultimately created more problems for me. I was not only being beaten, but felt guilt and shame because I wasn't holy or pure enough to have my prayers answered. This became very damaging to my spiritual life.

God did give people brains and talent to go to school and learn about the mind and the reasons we do what we do. He also gave them the desire to want to help human beings using these means. Counselors, psychologists, and psychiatrists are fulfilling their own life's mission. A good mental health professional will teach you how to think on your own. If you're continuing to see him or her for years and have a long list of problems or dilemmas that you've been saving since your last appointment, and you have no clue how to make your own decisions, it might be time to look for another counselor or start thinking for yourself.

One evening I was watching a television program on domestic violence. The guests included the sister of a well-known singer and her husband. They talked about what had happened in their marriage and what had created the violence. Because of his own insecurities (jealousy), he would build things up in his mind while he traveled until, when he returned home, his thoughts were now facts, and his spouse paid for it. See, lies affect abusers, too.

Sitting next to this blissfully happy couple was their minister, spiritual advisor, counselor, guru—whatever you want to call him—who had intervened on the wife's behalf. When the host of the program asked the spiritual advisor what he had said to finally reach this angry man, he replied, "I told him that the next time he hit her, I was going to come over to their house and show him what it felt like to be hit."

Naturally, the audience cheered. But, think about his statement long and hard. The audience clapped because they would be glad to see this man get some of his own medicine. I would, too, but—and this is a very big *but—why* would you treat violence with more violence? How could that possibly help?

He Is Out of Control

Have you ever wondered why your abuser has never hit you in front of a police officer or a neighbor? We say these men are out of control, but are they really? They *can* control themselves, which is why they're able to refrain from abuse in front of witnesses.

His abuse isn't a result of loss of self-control, but rather a demonstration of *full* control—over *you*. He can control himself; he just doesn't want to, and he doesn't see the need for it.

It also goes deeper than this. Men can lash out, hit, swear, or kick the dog. Women internalize. Rather than try to punish our abuser, we punish ourselves. We might drink to the point of becoming an alcoholic, take drugs to numb our pain and sorrow, become promiscuous and sleep with any man who will have us, or end our life—simply because we didn't reach out and seek help.

I've noticed when I talk before a group that the audience members are always more interested in the abuse I suffered than in the statistics about domestic violence. I can see people start to look around the room or squirm in their chairs. Why? As human beings, we're curious and always want to know about the grisly details surrounding some situation. We would rather hear about someone else's problems than learn how to solve our own.

I did a radio program a few years ago on domestic violence. The host of the show kept trying to get me to graphically reveal the abuse I had experienced. I would dodge the questions and try to explain why abused women react in the way they do. Every question that was put to me was answered in this way. It almost became a contest of wills between us.

I'm sure he wanted to increase his ratings, and I wanted to make the women in the listening audience stop feeling guilty about being hit. During the last few minutes of the program, I finally said, "Yes, my ex-husband beat me. He kicked, punched, and choked me." Who cares? It was the problem, not the solution.

Please heed the warning signs I've delineated in this chapter. They are so much more important than the beatings. If we are going to have healthy relationships, we need to really listen to the men we're with and not allow them or ourselves to play dangerous games.

I have a good friend who's been divorced for a number of years. The last thing he wants is to become involved. He's enjoying his freedom, and I used to see him at various social functions with different women. These women sometimes discussed their "relationship" with my friend with me. Their comments seemed to imply that he was getting serious with them.

One day I asked him what was going on. Was he playing a game with all these women?

He got really upset. "You know what, Di? I tell them at the very beginning that I'm not going to get involved for any reason. I make no promises, and I tell no lies."

These women all felt that they were so special that they could make my friend change his mind. They simply did not listen to what he told them, but instead, believed what they wanted to. That was four years ago, and he still isn't married.

I know women who have lived most of their lives being verbally abused by their mate. I witness it in stores. One time it was so terrible, I had to say something.

I overheard a man in the next aisle tell his wife, “I told you to price these coffee pots! That does not mean that you can continue to walk down the aisle when you’re finished. Now stand there until I tell you that you can move!”

I walked to their side of the aisle to see what this jerk looked like. He was a small, wimpy-looking man who was dressed like a nerd. I opened my purse and grabbed a card from a local shelter for battered women. As I handed it to her, I said, “Here, honey, you’re going to need this if you stay with this creep.”

It’s so sad to see couples who are 70 or 80 years old and the man is talking abusively to his wife. I’m sure these women have spent 50 years living like this. Why? Because they chose to. They didn’t respect themselves enough to tell their husband that his actions were not acceptable.

My mother had a good friend who actually hated her husband. He ranted and raved at her. He told her she was stupid, fat, ugly, and ignorant. She spent many hours crying on my mother’s shoulder. She had lived this life for more than 40 years!

One day while this man was moving a dresser, screaming at his wife that she wasn’t helping him properly, he dropped dead from a heart attack. This long-suffering wife then became the grieving widow. She felt guilty about the way she had talked about him even though it was the truth. She believed that her negative feelings toward this abusive man had caused his death. But it was *his* anger, not *her* thoughts that killed him.

When you learn to love yourself, you will not harm yourself. You will not accept the blame for other people’s problems. You will not make derogatory remarks about yourself or allow others to do so. You will not let another individual make decisions for you that will adversely affect your life. You will stop asking for others’ opinions. Only *you* know what is best for you. You will release friends from your life who make disparaging comments about you (even jokingly), and you will not date a man who doesn't respect your true qualities.

If your goal is inner peace, you need to associate with people who are striving for the same end. What may have worked ten years ago doesn't necessarily work today. You change. You grow. Once you get to the bottom of your anger and self-hatred, you cannot continue to surround yourself with negativity. When you've learned to truly love yourself, you will never ignore any warning signs the possible abuser reveals, because it will go against the natural instincts of your spirit.

CHAPTER 21

Our Own Warning Signs

If we women were to write down every single warning sign of the possibly abusive personality, we could fill an entire book. And even then, we'd miss some very telling signals. Of course, even if we did compile this huge tome, it would do absolutely no good if we ignored the signs that arose in the beginning stages of a relationship. If we are inclined to be attracted to the controlling person, chances are we're going to forge ahead and pretend that we can change this man.

Society, as a whole, has the tendency to focus on the abuser and his actions. "Watch out for this! Beware of that! This is how you deal with this situation!" While it is certainly prudent to be aware of certain traits, I've found that true independence and freedom come into play when we pay attention to *ourselves*. This is especially crucial if we are the types of women who have drifted from one abusive guy to another. We aren't paying attention, and we aren't growing or changing. What we have to do is be aware of our own warning signs—the ones that make us potential victims.

Below, I have pointed out a few signs that existed in my life that caused me to not only be *attracted to* an abuser, but to also draw him *to me.* Since most victims think along the same lines, I'm sure you'll recognize yourself (or someone you know) here.

The Need to Rescue

We hear or see something in a man that sets off our internal alarm. What do we do? Do we leave, recognizing that it is not our responsibility to try to "fix" someone? Or do we consider changing him or somehow living with the issue? The latter response is a warning sign—not of *his* potential for abuse, but of our own potential for falling into a "rescuer" mode. Yet, we never stop to ask ourselves why we would want to be in a relationship with someone with serious character flaws. When we attempt to change a person or save him, it is about *us*, not him. We believe it will make us seem noble or caring, but really, all it does is turn us into victims.

Self-Hatred

We reveal self-loathing through our spoken words. The mentally astute female does not condemn herself. When we make disparaging remarks about ourselves, this is a very loud and clear indication to the man of how we feel inside. He picks up on this trait very quickly. Be aware that the abuser is listening at all times. If we refuse to think poorly of ourselves, he'll understand that we won't allow him to speak negatively about us either—ever. Don't ever put yourself down. Instead, always affirm the positive. Author Louise Hay says that "our thoughts and words create our lives," and she's right!

Accepting Abuse

I consider dating to be a test. If you're seeing a person who leans toward control or verbal abuse, you can practice reacting in a self-serving way. Let's say that a man gets angry with you on a date and calls you horrible names. He'll watch to see just how much you're willing to tolerate. Perhaps you get very upset with him but forgive him when he apologizes. This is the "go-ahead" for him to not only do it again, but to progress to even more insulting and possibly physically abusive acts.

The type of man a healthy person wants to be with would never call a woman a degrading or insulting name—ever! It would not be a part of his personality. Remember something of great importance: Do not look at the apology—*look at the action that precipitated the apology.* Verbal abuse is not something that repentance can fix. It's a pattern that is only beginning and will grow worse if you're willing to accept it.

Lying to Ourselves

I was raised to believe that lying to someone was a sin: "Thou shalt not lie." But I didn't comprehend at the time that it's just as horrible to lie to ourselves. We basically commit a sin against our spirit when we refuse to acknowledge that a life filled with abuse is unacceptable.

This is why total and complete honesty is so important to our well-being. We may be able to lie to our friends ("I stay with him because I love him," "He needs me," "My children need a father," "He'll change"), but we can never totally lie to ourselves. When our spirit aches and we moan for some relief, we have to recognize that we are liars. We don't feel any great and compelling love for him, he doesn't need us, our children don't need a father who creates fear in their hearts, and he will never change. Lying to ourselves may not send us to hell, but we will live in hell while on Earth.

We believe that living in denial will rescue us. We look for our savior in bed while it actually resides within our soul. We may have walls up, believing they will protect us, but usually, the abuser is behind the walls we have built. We haven't protected ourselves; we've taken refuge with him at our side. We believe the lies thrown at us, while lying about our situation to ourselves. Why do you suppose we do this?

In effect, we believe it is much easier to maintain the status quo than to change. After we have been beaten numerous times, we have to acknowledge that this behavior is going to persist. It is easier for us to hope he will change, so we won't have to.

We may be very fearful of being alone or of struggling financially. Although these are very real fears, I've known too many women who have never worked, had no education, had children to feed and were terrified of losing custody of their offspring—and who took the bull by the horns and did what they had to do to find and maintain freedom. In other words, where there is a will, there is a way—regardless of what we believe.

We are also fearful, and shamed into worrying about what he will say about us if we leave. So we work harder at the big lie by staying and trying to be the perfect wife, and having a somewhat happy relationship—then we can leave! In this way, we won't look so horrible to others. Also, we believe he will then feel remorse because everything was going so well near the end.

A Dysfunctional Family History

Although we understand that we need to look at the abuser's family, it is equally important to view our own. If we lived in a dysfunctional home, we will have the tendency to repeat the patterns we learned there in our relationships. Don't pretend that your parents were Ozzie and Harriet when they weren't. It's perfectly fine to see them as they truly are—human beings with flaws. Just remember that they learned *their* behavior from parents, too.

I will always remember a young woman at a support group who was sporting a very painful-looking black eye, inflicted on her by her husband of one year. The group facilitator asked her about her childhood and how her parents interacted with each other. She claimed that her mom and dad were a loving and caring couple. But as she continued to talk, the truth came out. Her father had left her mother for another woman when she was 15 years old. Although they didn't divorce, he continued to live with the other woman across town. However, dear old Dad, on each payday, would come to their home and give his wife the money she needed to pay all her bills. The young woman believed that her parents were perfectly fine because they didn't argue during these visits. They sat down and had coffee and talked. In her mind, she had transformed them into a happily married couple.

In almost every story of the victim, there is a dysfunctional family lurking in the background. Whether verbal or physical abuse took place between the parents or between either or both parents and the child, it probably *did* exist. Denying the chain of iniquity in the family structure doesn't make it less real.

Fear of Being Alone

The fear of not being a part of a couple can make us willingly welcome any man into our lives who happens to appear on the scene. Maybe our girlfriends are all involved with someone, having a date every weekend, or taking part in group activities. We begin to think we're missing out on an important part of life by being single or dateless.

This is when we start settling for less than we would truly like. Our theory becomes: It sure beats staying at home all alone. Yet it's during our solitude that we learn about ourselves and discover the real woman inside. If we're with a man we don't even like, what are we learning except tolerance? From experience, I can tell you that there is no lonelier feeling than being on a date with a person you have absolutely nothing in common with and trying to pretend that you like him. It is boring and useless. There is a reason that the 12-step program, Alcoholics Anonymous, tells its members to take a year off from dating in order to get to know themselves. These are people who are in recovery, and so are we.

I could mention a hundred more warning signs, but they will do you no good if you don't heed them. The cycle of domestic violence will only stop when you really start paying attention to what the universe—and your own intuition—is telling you!

CHAPTER 22

The Mind of a Battered Woman

There is a huge difference between filing charges against a stranger who assaults you, and calling the police to arrest the man you loved (or still do love). Conflicting emotions can tear you apart. To understand these feelings of betrayal and confusion, let me present you with a scenario that is often all too real.

> *If I become truly frightened in a domestic abuse situation, my self-preservation will kick in and I'll pick up the phone and dial 911. The logical part of my brain understands that I could very well be killed or severely injured. The truth says, "This isn't right, and I want to be free!"*
>
> *The police arrive, and after seeing the house in shambles and the bruises on my body, they arrest my abuser, taking him away to spend the night in jail. I can sleep for one night without worrying about my safety, and the next morning I'm still very proud of my decision. I say to myself,* This should teach him a

lesson! *I call my supportive friends who know of the abuse and tell them what happened and how I handled it. They're also proud of me and offer encouragement.*

I prepare to go downtown to file a restraining order. The police officers have told me that this will offer additional protection should my abuser try to contact me. In a show of bravery, I reply, "Don't worry. I'll be there with bells on!" His violence has grown worse, and I've made too many empty threats. I'm finally going to get out of this very sick relationship.

I go to the courthouse and appear before the judge, explaining what took place and how frightened I am, thus requiring the court's refuge. I'm given the Order of Protection, but as I'm leaving the courtroom, I see something I wasn't expecting—my abuser is standing in the hallway, preparing to face the judge in his arraignment. He stares at me with a look of contempt and total hatred. I know that he'd kill me if he could.

I understand that I've done the right thing, but something keeps nagging at my thoughts. What is it? As I think about recent events, I realize that I'm worried about my abuser's disapproval of me. I've lived only for his favor, and now it's gone. This creates enormous fear inside me.

What should I do? I know—I'll telephone him later in the day and explain why I called the police. I'll feel better if I know he understands my motives. We can both be happy then. But when he hears my voice, he tells me to go to hell and hangs up on me. I panic when I realize how angry he is with me. Now what do I do?

The evening is very long and lonely. I know that

he beat me on a regular basis when we were living together, but at least I wasn't sitting here by myself with nothing to do except feel guilty and scared. I finally go to bed, but instead of sleeping, I begin to plan. I think of lies—fabricated reasons I can make up to get him on my side. I'll create a story about something that happened the day he abused me that kept me from thinking clearly. I'll let him know that there will never be another woman who will love him as much as I do. And just to show him how serious I am, I'll call the police and ask them to drop the charges. However, when I call, the police tell me it is now out of my hands and is a matter for the courts.

In a panic, the next day I drive to his place of employment and wait until he gets off work. I run to his car when I see him approaching and tell him I'm sorry—I don't know what got into me—I love him so much—I'm miserable without him. I point out that we have a history together—does he want to throw it all away?

As I cry and plead, using all of my little-girl ploys, he looks at me warily. I almost have him back. Wait! I have another idea. Let me cook you your favorite meal tonight—a romantic dinner for two, just like old times. He reluctantly agrees, and I'm relieved because I no longer have this horrible guilt nagging at me, and I once again have his approval.

He is nice to me during the 14 days before his appearance to face domestic violence charges. In court, I stand before the judge and proclaim that we had a quarrel that got out of hand, and I feel that what goes on in our family should be a private matter, not something for the courts to decide. The judge disagrees and fines him. Because of my guilt, I tell

> *my abuser that I'll pay the fine, which seems to dissipate much of his anger.*
>
> *Relieved that this unnecessary embarrassment is behind us, we celebrate that evening with a bottle of wine. And then, remembering the night he spent in jail because of me—he once again beats me.*

I know this sounds far-fetched, but it isn't. This horrendous scenario happens all the time. When a woman who has been emotionally and physically dependent on a man stands up for her rights, her initial sense of power is almost immediately replaced by an almost overwhelming sense of fear. The dynamics of the relationship have changed—but *she* has not. At some level, she still needs his approval and the dubious security of the relationship. She fears his rejection more than the abuse.

Do you see yourself in this woman? If you do, there is something very important you need to understand—you have never truly had the abuser's approval. In an attempt to rewrite your history with him, you have built up the fantasy that someday his good graces will be bestowed upon you—regardless of what has happened in the past. You are moving in circles, driven by fear.

You have to go within to extricate yourself from this cycle. You have to address the basis of your fears, which could be financial, emotional, social, physical, or psychological. Which is worse—confronting his anger and violence over and over again, wondering when the next explosion is going to occur and knowing that this will go on for the rest of your life; or leaving this toxic relationship and working through the *temporary* pain and fear in order to create a sane life for yourself?

What thoughts go through your mind when you try to emotionally detach from your abuser and start to think about leaving him? Do you focus on material comforts instead of peace of mind? Is your idea of security a roof over your head, even though it covers a violent household? What does the word *security* mean to you?

Are you afraid to call the police, embarrassed by what the neighbors will think? Are you frightened that once you take a stand, others will think you're a fool when you let him come back? Haven't you been hiding the abuse because you aren't ready to leave him yet? Do you worry that exposing the truth will force you into making a decision?

You know your life will change if you leave him. Aren't you afraid of making your own decisions and being responsible for yourself and your children? Don't you really want him to take care of you and take charge of your life? You don't think you can handle the responsibilities of an adult, do you? Isn't it your belief that you will fail if you try to make it on your own?

Has someone in your past made you feel that you don't deserve to be treated fairly? You weren't born with this sense of unworthiness, were you? You've given your power away for most of your life because of this belief—right? You're scared to death to stand up to those people you believe have all the strength, aren't you? And don't you tell yourself that "the meek shall inherit the earth"?

You believe that unless a woman is bruised, she isn't a victim of domestic violence, don't you? You don't think that words can destroy you just as much as physical blows. You find your strength in being submissive and not defending yourself because he doesn't really mean the horrible things he says to and about you. It will keep your family together if you just ignore his actions, won't it?

You like to use his addiction to alcohol or drugs as an excuse for the abuse. "If he would just stop drinking, we wouldn't have a problem." This makes it easier to ignore his actions, while pointing your finger at an inanimate object such as a liquor bottle, and cursing it. After all, blaming the *addiction* is better than blaming *him*. He can't help what he does, can he? The poor thing was drunk, and he lost control. And your friends may look upon him with more sympathy if they think he has a "disease." This also makes you feel better, too, doesn't it, because you're married to a man who is sick, rather than just mean?

You've called shelters to find a support group for him, even though he hasn't expressed a need or desire to get help. But you know you can force him into recovery, whether he wants it or not! You're going to make this happen, come hell or high water. You are going to make this man become your knight in shining armor. He has to change because it takes too much work for you to change yourself. And you'll feel more powerful being the one who brought about this drastic rebirth once he becomes the man you've always dreamed of. This isn't just about him, is it? Your ego is in there somewhere.

Maybe you assume that his abuse is a spiritual problem—it's Satan's fault! Now you can offer up prayers, get him delivered from the hands of the enemy, have him anointed with oil, and perform an exorcism. The forces of evil have been working against him, stealing his rightful standing before God. You've preached God's word to him at every opportunity, pointing out his sin—which isn't really *his* sin at all. He's just been at the mercy of the devil.

Don't you find it impossible to believe that he doesn't know how to love? You make excuses for his unloving actions, don't you? Isn't it easier to blame his background and family than to recognize that he's simply a very violent and angry man? Haven't you found that it gives you a reason to keep hanging on?

You've made a lot of threats, and don't you want to

believe that he lives in fear of them? You actually think that you've reached him this time. It gives you a sense of power to scare him into thinking that you'll leave him if he ever hits you again. And every time you go through this old and tired routine, you still have faith, don't you?

Once you've found the strength to leave him, you sit by the phone, praying he'll call to offer an apology or excuse. Aren't you frightened beyond belief that he won't call? Don't you hope that he's lonely and pining for you? Are you thinking, *Maybe I pushed it too far this time; what if he calls my bluff and doesn't come back?*

Have you become addicted to havoc? You have no idea what a normal, healthy relationship is. All you understand is arguments, lies, broken promises, betrayal, and abuse. Unless there is fighting, and then making up, you don't feel like you're in a meaningful relationship.

You don't know the difference between love and obsession—right? To you, they're the same things. You think you have to work for love and prove yourself to be worthy of it.

When you're alone, you secretly question how you've brought out these bad qualities in him, don't you? You think that there's something very wrong with you that makes him act the way he does. You have no doubt that if he had become involved with another woman, he would be different. You analyze what is wrong with you and how you can fix yourself.

You feel you must compete with other women he has compared you to. You just don't measure up to them. You work very hard on improving yourself so he'll give you the glowing compliments he throws their way. You don't understand that a wife doesn't have to compete with other women, do you? You've accepted a second-place position—behind virtual strangers.

You really believe that meeting all of his demands will

make you a better wife. Doesn't it give you a feeling of righteousness when you're subservient? And don't you know for certain that God will bless you for your attempts? After all, God is love! He'll view you as a holier woman if you don't leave a man who beats you. You believe that the women in your church look up to you for your steadfastness with the Lord. You think submission is Godly—regardless of how it makes you feel.

You feel like you can't live without him—your life source is found in this man who chokes, slaps, kicks, punches, rapes, yells, and throws you into walls. You don't believe for one moment that he could someday kill you. Not him! Not this man that you think you love!

Am I too blunt for your comfort level? It took someone being very candid and dogmatic to make me see the truth instead of my perceived reality. I needed the clarity of potent words to finally be my wake-up call. If I had continued to ignore and deny my life while minimizing the abuse—I probably wouldn't be alive today!

Successfully abandoning an abusive situation requires more than a police report or a court order. Until you reject the role assigned to you by the abuser and find your own identity, you will leave, only to return. Your worth as a person has been overshadowed by the lies your abuser has told you, the hatred he feels for you, and your own lack of self-respect.

If you see yourself in this chapter, you know it's time to get help. You're the only one who can make that decision, but it will be the most important decision you will ever make. The cliché that life is short is a reality. Why waste one more day dancing around issues? It's important to stay in tune with your heartbeat, and only you know the rhythm of your life. You can escape a violent relationship if you have the will to do so.

I had to ask myself what kind of pay-off I was getting by staying with my abuser. So do you. *What is it?* If you are honest with yourself, you'll find the answer to that question. If there wasn't some kind of reward (to your way of thinking), you wouldn't stay. You have to get to the bottom of your reasoning and your issues to escape from the domestic violence cycle. Your life could very well depend on it. The truth won't hurt you as much as his blows do.

You must dig, scratch, climb, or run. Do whatever it takes to find the real you. Do what is important to you—no matter what. You're worth it. Listen to your inner voice.

CHAPTER 23

The Effects of Domestic Violence on Our Children

Domestic violence is not just a private matter between two adults. It also affects the other members of the family—especially our children. The kids are helpless witnesses to the "traumatic bonding" that takes place when love and abuse are commingled. One day they see Mom and Dad going through the honeymoon phase, and everything seems as if it's going to work out for the best. But, the following day, Dad could be in one of his rages and hit Mom.

Eventually, our children begin to resent us for raising them in this hostile environment. They may start engaging in destructive and dangerous behavior themselves in an effort to escape the home situation, further adding to the family's problems.

And, should they find themselves involved in this same kind of abusive relationship, they will be less likely to question it. Studies have shown that when children grow into adults, they imitate and identify with the lifestyle in which they were raised. Therefore, if they were reared in a family where domestic violence was considered the norm, they may consider abuse as love and be more likely to engage in an abusive relationship themselves. The cycle of domestic violence has taken on a life of its own, repeating itself through the generations.

In talking with many victims and by evaluating my own upbringing, I have tried to analyze what conditions could predispose someone to be a future victim. As a result, I have developed a list of 12 questions to help you assess the interactions within your family, highlighting potential danger areas.

1. When your daughter approaches you with a question, are the first words out of your mouth, "Go ask your father"?

When you always put the male in the position of having all the answers, this can be compared to telling your child that your opinion is not valuable. Surely you too have an opinion!

This mode of behavior also results in the loss of a great opportunity to communicate. There is a reason your child came to you with a question—she wanted *your* answers. If she had wanted to speak with her father, she would have gone to him.

2. Do you allow your spouse or partner to make insulting comments about your daughter or son?

Are you allowing this to occur because you're expecting approval from your mate? What about your children's feelings? These destructive remarks will lower their self-esteem and make them resent you for not defending them. Where are your children supposed to go for support, if not to you? You will harm, if not destroy, their spirit if you allow this to take place. And when they reach adulthood, they could very well seek out a mate who will treat them in the same way. Thus, the cycle will continue.

3. Do you discourage your children from making decisions on their own?

Have you ever met grown women who rely on others for every decision regarding their lives? They get on the phone in a panic, making numerous calls to friends to ask what they should do about this or that. If you were to look into their background, chances are that they had parents who controlled their every move. As a result, they never learned how to make decisions for themselves.

As a parent, there has to come a time when you begin to loosen the apron strings. If you don't allow your children to make choices in their teen years, they will mistrust their own intelligence and decision-making skills. Instead, they may be drawn to a controlling, possibly abusive mate who will make their decisions for them. Remember that this is one of the signs abusers will look for—a person they will be able to control and manipulate.

4. Do you discourage your child from being self-supporting and financially independent?

This warning sign is more common for daughters than sons. When you raise your daughter to believe she doesn't need to be able to support herself, but should instead rely on a man to provide for her, you're setting her up to either be dependent on a spouse for the rest of her life or to struggle financially if she never marries. If she should marry an abuser, she will be far more likely to remain in the relationship, since she is financially dependent on him. You should encourage your daughters to become financially independent, even if they do plan to marry.

5. Do you snoop through your children's private belongings, not allowing them any privacy?

Every human being deserves to have areas in their personal life that others don't have access to. Your children's notes, journals, or letters should be off-limits to your snooping eyes. The distrust you are showing is not an element of love, but a demonstration of control. As a result, you are setting them up to accept this behavior from other people "in the name of love."

6. When your kids ask if they can do something or go somewhere, is "No" your first response?

I can tell you from personal experience that this tendency creates frustration and sometimes rage. When I was a teenager, every time I asked my father if I could go somewhere with my friends, there was a ritual we had to go through. He would say no, and I would have to beg and sometimes cry while pleading my case. Then he would tell me how ugly I was when I cried. Only after all this torment was I given permission to go out. If you exert this kind of control and domination over your children, you can expect rebellion and hostility in return, which will ultimately damage your relationship with them.

7. Do you treat members of the opposite sex with disrespect?

If Dad is abusive and calls all women degrading names, or if Mom behaves as though all men are untrustworthy, their sons will repeat this offense or their daughters will accept it from other men. If you want your offspring to have respect for others, you must set the example.

8. If you're divorced or separated from your mate, do you make disparaging comments about him?

You're angry with your former spouse and want the world to know. You also believe that your hostility and rage toward him should be shared. You think that your children should feel the same way you do, and you're going to make sure they do.

What you don't understand is this: Your relationship with your mate should be kept separate from your children's relationship with them. Otherwise, it will be extremely destructive and confusing to the children involved. You need to let them form their own bonds, regardless of how you feel. By placing them in the middle of an emotional battleground, their ability to develop stable relationships in the future could be affected.

9. Are you making your child the family scapegoat?

This happens very often in dysfunctional families. Mom and Dad aren't able to deal with the problem that exists between them as a couple, so they will find a victim to put in its place. Suddenly, one child is chosen to represent every disaster that happens. She (or he) is now blamed for every problem within the family and even starts to believe what is being said. As a result, the child ends up with a complete lack of self-esteem.

Sometimes, the child starts to think she should fix the situation, which is, of course, impossible. Failing in the role as peacemaker, this child then spends her entire adult life trying to save the world and every abusive person she meets in order to feel worthwhile. The focus is on making everyone else happy—even at the expense of her own happiness.

10. Do you allow your child to express her opinion?

Normally, if you meet an adult who's afraid to speak up, you'll find a family in her background that expected her to stifle her opinions, also. If she tried to offer up her thoughts, she was either laughed at or told to be quiet. Soon, she can no longer risk venturing into this degrading territory. As an adult, she has turned into a doormat.

By allowing your child to voice her opinions, she will gain more confidence in her judgment and intelligence, thereby building her self-respect and self-worth.

11. Do you go into rages or verbal tirades?

Notice what happens when you fly off the handle. Friends and family members will run and hide, or try to avoid you at all costs. This was your ultimate goal, right? Controlling others with your actions? This dubious power does not make you appear intelligent or wise, only abusive. You must learn to control this demeaning behavior—not only for your own sake, but for the sake of your children, who are watching—and learning.

12. Do you truly listen to your children when they talk to you?

This doesn't mean pretending to listen, just waiting for a break in the conversation so you can interject your opinion. This means listening to your children's words and really taking heed of what they're saying. This gives you the chance to learn a great deal about their thought processes and current state of mind, and also lets them know that you're an available source of support. If *you* don't make yourself accessible to them, they will find someone else who is willing to listen—and it could be an individual who doesn't have their best interests at heart.

None of us is a perfect parent; we all make mistakes while raising our children. But what's important is that we try our best. And if we've made major mistakes because of our own dysfunctional upbringing, we can still undo the damage. We can reach out to our kids and tell them we love and care about them. We can take the time to communicate with them on their level, without condemnation, so they feel validated. We don't have to perpetuate negative patterns.

If we've never experienced parental love, it may be difficult to know how to show it. This is one reason shelters for battered women offer parenting classes. These women need to be taught how to be mothers. They didn't have a role model to teach them how to care for a child. But they can learn, and so can we.

If we are living with an abuser, we should analyze the damage the violence is doing to our children. If we continue to live with abuse, we are teaching our children that it is acceptable. Although we would never intentionally raise our children to be abusers or victims, we might be doing so unintentionally.

The fact of the matter is: *If we want to break the cycle of domestic violence and protect our children, the process must begin with us.*

CHAPTER 24

Finding Our True Essence Through Therapy

When we seek our True Self, we are entering into the deepest part of our being. It is the area of our soul that is able to guide, teach, love, and reach out to others. Basically, it is the essence of us, the aura we leave behind that comforts and helps others find their personal path. It is the serenity that others perceive when they speak with us, and it creates a longing within them to find their own inner peace and tranquillity.

Many victims of abuse ask, "How can I find my essence, or my True Self? I've tried, but I seem to stay exactly where I am—stuck in a life of depression, dependency, and misery, attracting one loser after another."

The answer is simple—through therapy sessions. From experience, I can assure you that counseling will change your outlook about life—virtually every aspect of it. Therapy is much more than a walk down memory lane; it's a very enlightening exploration of why you respond the way you do; why you only react to circumstances instead of acting to change them; how you've grasped at ideas that weren't yours, but another's; and how to stop engaging in destructive actions that keep you in the victim mode. When you begin to find your True Self, you will wonder why you waited so long to accept the help that's available.

You may have been told that all psychologists are humanistic or atheists and will infiltrate your mind with thoughts that go against God. Maybe you've heard that it's dangerous to turn control over to a stranger. Or perhaps your family has taught you to keep the family secrets to yourself and not air your dirty laundry for others to see. If you're still living with an abuser, you might worry that the therapist will urge you to take a course you're not yet willing to follow. Although these may seem like valid points, I can tell you that these excuses aren't well founded.

It's extremely important to find a qualified therapist with a degree in counseling—and not just a shingle hanging on the front door. And, just because someone has a degree doesn't necessarily mean that this person will be right for you. Some counselors can be condemning and too dogmatic, which will only serve to make you feel worse than you do now. You may not trust men in general and feel uneasy speaking with one and decide that a female counselor would be better. Whatever the case, it's your prerogative to change therapists if you aren't comfortable. You certainly don't want to deal with someone you don't really like or are unable to open up to. Trust your instincts.

One reason for not seeking help from a therapist is because our lives and problems seem too overwhelming. How in the world could we sift through so much? The effort required doesn't seem worth it. It would be much easier to read books, talk with friends, or handle our problems on our own, in our own way. But while reading books about our situation can give us information, and talking our problems over with friends can provide some support, it isn't enough.

We need the assistance of a trained counselor to help us identify the *real* problems, analyze them individually, and learn new techniques to successfully deal with them.

Another problem could be that the victim isn't ready to leave her abuser and is fearful that he'll discover she's talking with a therapist. Qualified professionals will never divulge any information about their patients, so any trick the abuser tries to use to elicit information won't work. If the abuser follows or stalks you, tell him you're going to therapy to deal with your own problem areas and that it has nothing to do with him. I've seen this tactic really work on several occasions, since the abuser naturally thinks that it's the other person who needs help.

Many women have told me that they simply can't afford counseling because leaving the abuser meant losing money, furniture, their home, and sometimes their job. Because our society understands this dilemma, they have made resources available to assist us. Clinics have sliding-fee scales, and some of the social services offer free counseling. You just have to be patient and find the right resource. In the meantime, find a support group for victims of domestic violence, which will help you stay strong and not be tempted to return to the abuser. Call a local shelter and talk with one of the volunteers as soon as possible!

If you still think you can't afford counseling, remember what the abusive situation is costing you: your peace of mind, your health, and your family stability. You'll realize that the financial cost of therapy may be far less than the price paid for not going.

I've also noticed that some women who say they can't afford to continue therapy have really reached a point in counseling that is making them uneasy. They may be at a crossroads and realize that they must either take a step forward toward wellness or fall back into the life of pain they were trying to escape. If you stop therapy as soon as it becomes painful for you, your growth will stagnate. Anger is one of the expected phases you will experience along the way, and it usually takes place right before the healing and realization process begins—so stick it out.

Time commitments are also used as reasons to avoid seeking help. Ask yourself these questions: "How much *time* have you spent trying to reason with your abuser? How much *time* did you have to take out of your busy schedule to visit a doctor? Did you miss *time* at work because of emotional and physical trauma?" Most important, "Why will you spend *time* trying to rescue a man who has beaten you, but not take the *time* to save yourself?"

What You Can Expect in Therapy

Therapy is not frightening; it's the exact opposite. On your first visit, the doctor, counselor, or therapist will ask you questions about your employment and your closest living relative (for emergency or contact information—not to check into your past). You will provide a brief medical history and your reasons for contacting him or her. You may not be ready to open up about your real issues at this point in time, but you've taken the first step. Now, that isn't too intimidating, is it?

On your second visit, you will be given the opportunity to share what is bothering you, or the other thoughts you've had since your last session (trust me, you'll have many). You may have written down questions so you won't forget anything.

If you are hesitant about sharing too much at first, the counselor will guide you with questions, which helps you relax. But remember that he or she is actually listening to what you say! And often, the counselor will pick up on key words that you have uttered unthinkingly.

For example, Bob, my therapist, asked me why I hadn't done a certain thing, and I casually replied, "Oh, I'm not allowed to do that." I thought nothing of my statement and continued to talk, but he stopped me and made me back up. "You aren't *allowed* to? Did you just hear what you said? Are you a child or a grown woman? Why would you let a man treat you like a little girl and tell you that you're not *allowed* to do something?"

His questions made me look back at my relationship with John and realize that the pattern for abuse was set when I gave him the right to control my life. Eventually I learned that my willingness to grant John that power was fostered by my belief that I wasn't smart enough to be responsible for my own life—but it took probing questions from my therapist to help me come to this realization.

Your insights are not limited by the walls of your therapist's office. After a session, you'll continue to analyze why you react in certain ways, how your past has affected your present life, and most important, why you were attracted to and have continued to stay with an abusive man. But the greatest blessing is the change that begins to take place inside your mind and spirit. It's like magic, and it feels absolutely wonderful! There is nothing like knowledge to help you regain the power you've had stolen—or have given away—unknowingly.

With the help of a dedicated, intelligent, and compassionate therapist, I've moved on to lead a very happy and productive life. And so can *you*.

Today is the day you can make the call that could change your life!

CHAPTER 25

Discovering Our Passion

Passion is an interesting subject because it's one of the outward ways in which we can express our deepest self. We can be passionate about work or passionate about our children. Passion isn't always about men or sex. And remarkably, our passions can change with time and age. As we get to know ourselves better, our interests and ideas will often shift.

Often, people will find their new passion through tragedy or a life-changing event. It will be something they would have never asked for, but when it took place, they realized that a new blessing had come into their lives that could serve as a source of healing.

I met a middle-aged couple who bought vans and reconstructed them for the handicapped. Their work in this area was initiated when their 19-year-old son was killed in a skiing accident. He had broken his neck and they knew, had he lived, that he would have been in a wheelchair for the remainder of his life. So, their healing took place when they were able to help others in this situation.

Christopher Reeve is another example. Who would have dreamed that "Superman" would end up being a spokesperson for the disabled? Mary Fisher is another person with a mission. Infected with AIDS by her former, now-deceased husband, she has refused to wallow in self-pity but has made a concentrated effort to educate the public about HIV and AIDS.

What about *us?* Will we remain steeped in our anger, sorrow, regrets, and self-pity, or will we move on? Do we continue to talk ad nauseam to everybody about what "he" did and how he did it and how awful it was—or do we move past it and chalk it up to a lesson well learned? Can we move ahead, or do we remain stalled, frozen in time?

We don't have to become an advocate of domestic violence because we've escaped from our own situation. We may prefer not to ever speak of it again. But I've found that one of the best ways to get over the trauma is to find a passion that takes up our devotion and efforts. When we do so, we focus on the hopeful present instead of the depressing past.

Part of healing is using our talents and desires to make our lives a success. I've found that God usually gives us talent and drive in our lives intermingled, so to speak, to help us achieve our goals. In other words, if we have the drive to do something, we normally have the talent, too.

When you discover your passion, you will notice that you are your happiest while doing it. Your life will run much more smoothly because you are on your true path. Suddenly, the little things that used to irritate you will no longer bother you in the slightest. You won't have time for negativity because your energy is being directed toward your passion.

When we meet people who are passionate, we are drawn to their energy. They express a great drive that makes them appealing. They have the courage to make their dreams a reality. They don't attain their goals because they are smarter than we are, but because they care so deeply and have the courage to make their dreams come true.

Often I will meet highly educated women who were on the road to achieving their goals, only to see them throw their dreams away due to the protestations made by an abusive partner. If he didn't insist on her quitting her job, his demands on her spirit caused so much anxiety that she wasn't able to perform her job and was fired. Her energies were directed toward the wrong areas. Basically, she lost her passion.

As you look back on your childhood, recall what you wanted to be when you grew up. This is usually an indication of your passion. Did you love to paint? Did you have a talent for music? Did you spend hours writing poetry? Were you designing dresses for your dolls? Did you have visions of becoming an actress? Was your teacher an example of what you wanted to be? Did you spend hours in your bedroom reading books, thinking of becoming a writer?

Did you grow up to become what you dreamed of, but found it to be undesirable? Then chances are, you aren't truly living your passion. Have you remained in this profession because of fear of change or fear of a decrease in salary? Have you forgotten all the famous people who changed careers midstream, in their 40s and 50s, who went on to become well known for other endeavors? I'm certain they experienced some self-doubt, too, but their success lay in the courage to keep pressing forward.

If we take a small amount of time each day to pursue our passion, our efforts will eventually pay off. We have to make a determined effort to realistically treat our passion as a second job without pay. This may require us to get out of bed each morning an hour earlier than normal, give up certain social events, learn to say no to friends, and focus our energy on what we know is most important. We will begin to feel so driven to follow our dreams that we don't find the past important any longer. We are focused on the future.

Don't allow the old thoughts to filter into your mind that try to tell you to give up. So many times while writing this book, I heard my father's voice telling me, "Who do you think you are trying to help people when you're so screwed up yourself!" I fought against these old mental tapes daily until I finally pressed the stop button. I was no longer trying to prove anything to *him;* I just wanted to help other women.

I've spoken with many survivors of domestic violence who seem to have a problem releasing their anger. In retrospect, their anger has become their passion. When we find our *true* passion, this situation dissipates. We don't have energy to spend on rage anymore. When we wake up each morning, our thoughts will be directed toward our goals. Our spirit leads us to positive actions that will guide us. We will find ourselves trying to return to feelings of anger and then we'll catch ourselves and put a stop to such negativity.

When we put as much energy into our passion as we did trying to make an abusive relationship work, we are destined for success. Everything seems to suddenly go smoothly, we have more energy, and we're at peace with ourselves. How different from what we experienced in the past! I believe this is our Higher Power's way of telling us that we're on the right path.

Is our life mission and passion one in the same? I believe they are. One is a very strong indication of the other. Our mission usually includes our passion, and vice versa. We experience a certain high while working toward our ideal; and we won't allow society, people, books, or anything else to deter us from attaining our goal.

The way to live a passionate life is to just put one foot in front of the other, plan, think, ask advice, and move forward. The good life is right in front of you—just reach for it!

CHAPTER 26

Turning to a Higher Power

Prayer As a Power for Change

We must never underestimate the power of prayer. It is a very effective tool—one that can give us the strength to make positive changes in our life. But to access this Higher Power, we must be open to It, actively seek Its source, and then be willing to make the necessary alterations. Spirituality is about growth, not regression. Prayer can show us the changes we must make, but it is up to us to implement them.

We have to be a willing vessel. We ask, and then we respond to the answers in a way that transforms us into more spiritual beings. If we were sitting in a classroom and asked the instructor a question but didn't listen to his answer, we wouldn't learn. In the same way, we learn to listen to God, The Great Instructor.

Many survivors of domestic violence want to steer clear or any organized religion, afraid of being put back in a situation where they are being told how to think, what to do, and how to live their lives. But we don't have to sit in a building to pray, and we don't have to wait for someone to lead us to our Higher Power. We can seek Him (or Her) in our own way.

How do we get in touch with our Higher Power (or whatever name you wish to call it)? We simply open ourselves up to Him, making ourselves ready to receive His love and blessings. The love and support we will receive is unconditional and ever-present. Our very existence makes us worthy of that love, and the only person who can stop it from coming to us is ourselves.

We must take the first step and tear down the barriers that keep us from reaching out. Many of us believe we are unworthy of God's love. After all, didn't our abuser tell us time and time again what a terrible person we were, and how no one would ever love us? Or perhaps it was our family who made us feel inadequate or unworthy.

In any case, we must take decisive action. I always tell victims of domestic violence to take every negative statement made to them or about them, and throw them out and start with a clean slate. Consider every horrible indictment a lie that was created to bring you under control and manipulate you into submission. Pull the old tapes from your mind and replace them with new ones that tell you how wonderful you are and how justified you are in receiving the very best. Argue with the old voices and confront their validity, and you'll find that they eventually go away and die a slow death, never to return.

Another barrier is shame—the shame we feel about actions in our past, believing that they were so terrible that we don't deserve forgiveness. Recognizing that, we must take the next step and forgive ourselves for what we've done—or haven't done—in the past. We made our mistakes because we didn't know any better or were operating under false or erroneous assumptions—not because we were bad people. The past can't be undone, so we must accept it as a part of our life and then move on. These painful events were lessons. Their purpose was to get us to where we are right now, at this moment. Our experiences were meant to instruct and guide us, not punish us.

The final barrier is holding on to hate—the resentment we feel toward those who have abused us. As difficult as it may seem, *we must forgive those who have hurt us!* This doesn't require a face-to-face meeting with our abuser. It takes place in our hearts. We recognize the harm the abuser did to us, and then we let it go. By holding on to the anger, we are still allowing our abuser to influence our life. And it's impossible to have hate or anger residing in the same house as God's love. We must turn all the anger over to Him, which will create and open space for the blessings that He has promised us.

Once we've removed these barriers, then the strength and blessings from our Higher Power can reach us, and doors will be opened. Because we're able to accept and love ourselves, we are able to embrace the love and blessings of our Higher Power. We become better people—the individuals we were destined to be—and we find the strength to achieve goals that we thought were unattainable. We can also serve as a beacon of light for others who are searching for the same strength we have found.

When I first began writing this book, I was filled with self-doubt. What if what I had to say had no value? What if I lacked the gift to put my thoughts and feelings into words? What if I didn't have the ability to finish what seemed to be a monumental, and at times, heart-wrenching task?

To overcome these fears, I went through a ritual each time I faced the computer keyboard. I would breathe deeply, relax, and pray for guidance. Some days just flew by. I felt I had only been writing for one hour, when it had actually been five or six. And the words! I had to question where the wisdom was coming from. At times, I actually grew somewhat frightened and would stay away from the computer, not returning for several days. It took some time for me to realize that this was Divine Intervention taking place, allowing me the time and space to gather my thoughts. I truly felt that my Higher Power was working to lead and guide me during the writing of this book.

You Are Blessed

Believe me, I'm no different from you. I don't possess any great strength or powers that you don't, and I'm not luckier than you are. I'm just one of many women who have learned to listen. I've opened myself up to God's direction, and rely on His support and wisdom. That, in turn, gives me the ability to achieve my goals.

There is a reason why this book has crossed your path. There are no such things as coincidences. Events occur for a reason, and people and reading materials come into our lives when we need them most ("When the student is ready, the teacher will come"). It is my profound hope that this book will be a blessing for you—a step toward growth and inner knowing, and another opportunity to find fulfillment.

If I could reach out and hug you and convince you just how wonderful and worthy you truly are, I would cherish the chance to do so. If it would help for me to stand on a rooftop and loudly proclaim that you are loved, I'd be pulling my ladder out of storage. If I was able to wipe away your tears and tell you that I understand how you feel and what you're going through, and offer the hope that you *can* and *will* work through your heartache, I would be knocking on your front door right now. I would tell you that you're a blessing just because you're alive.

But because I am only one woman and can't be there physically to speak with you, I want to use another method to show you that you're a blessing and are blessed.

Close your eyes and create a picture in your mind of what your life should and could become. Visualize yourself walking into a room filled with people who are strangers to you. Your posture is straight and your head is held high. Your most compelling feature is your warm and shining smile, which reaches all the way to your eyes. You greet each person with a firm handshake, speaking openly and showing real interest in what they're saying. You make them feel special with your words and actions, and in return, they are drawn to you. You radiate an aura of love, compassion, vitality, and serenity. They want to learn your secret to life, hoping it will rub off on them.

Unbeknownst to you, there are several women standing in the corner whispering, "Did you know that she was married to a man who beat her at one time?" The other women pull back in shock. "You must be kidding—her? That's impossible to fathom. She must have tapped in to a secret part of the universe, or a miracle took place for her to come out of it in such great shape. Let's go talk to her and find out how she did it!"

What is the *secret* we've unearthed that causes complete strangers to seek out our company? We discovered our inner selves—we put the lies behind us and found the truth. We've learned that self-love is a very effective and powerful tool.

Blessings flow both ways once the barriers are torn down. We are being a blessing to others as we share, but we are also the ones who are blessed when we openly and truthfully give of ourselves to help heal our world.

You can become the woman in the vision. You can be both loved and loving. You can serve as a blessing to others, and be blessed yourself. You can comprehend life's lessons and then use them to help others. With the help of your Higher Power, you will become a strong, whole woman, and then help others find their own strength.

Your blessed life is predestined for you; it is just waiting for you to discover it. Start that journey now and don't look back. Keep your eyes focused forward and expect great and wonderful things to happen. Your Higher Power will walk beside you and guide you through each step. Move out into the world and find your own peace and tranquillity. I'm so excited for you!

Endnotes

1. Page 3. "Female Victims of Violent Crime," Washington, D.C. U.S. Department of Justice, 1991.

2. Page 114. Angela Browne, *When Battered Women Kill,* New York, NY: The Free Press, 1987.

3. "Over 50 percent of all women will experience physical violence in intimate relationships. For about 25 percent of them, the battering will be regular and ongoing." (Remarks by Judge Richard. Lee Price at "Love and Violence: Victims and Perpetrators," New York City Coalition for Women's Mental Health, January 1991).

4. According to Anna Wilson, editor of *Introduction to Homicide: The Victim/Offender,* Cincinnati, OH: Anderson Publishing Co., 1993, p. 3, "Most prevalence-rate studies estimate that 28 percent of all adult women in a relationship are victims of domestic violence on an annual basis."

5. Almost seven years ago, the Surgeon General of the United States warned that violence was the number-one public health risk to adult women in the United States. Unfortunately, four years later, it still remains the leading cause of injuries to

women ages 15 to 44 (June 1992), more common than automobile accidents, mugging, and cancer deaths combined! (Violence Against Women, A Majority Staff Report, Committee on the Judiciary, United States Senate, 102nd Congress, October 1992, p. 3.

6. "Battering is the major cause of injury to women, resulting in about one million visits annually to physicians," reports Michael Dowd in "Is the Law Abusing Women?" *Woman's Day,* September 13, 1988, p. 117.

Self-Help Resources

The following list of resources can be used to access information on a variety of issues. The addresses and telephone numbers listed are for the national headquarters; look in your local yellow pages under "Community Services" for resources closer to your area.

In addition to the following groups, other self-help organizations may be available in your area to assist your healing and recovery for a particular life crisis not listed here. Consult your telephone directory, call a counseling center or help line near you, or contact:

Attorney Referral Network
(800) 624-8846

National Self-Help Clearinghouse
25 West 43rd St., Room 620
New York, NY 10036
(800) 952-2075

AIDS

AIDS Hotline
(800) 342-2437

Children with AIDS (CWA) Project of America
(800) 866-AIDS (24-hour hotline)

The Names Project – AIDS Quilt
(800) 872-6263

National AIDS Network
(800) 342-2437

Project Inform
19655 Market St., Ste. 220
San Francisco, CA 94103
(415) 558-8669

PWA Coalition
50 W. 17th St.
New York, NY 10011

Spanish AIDS Hotline
(800) 344-7432

TDD (Hearing Impaired) AIDS Hotline
(800) 243-7889

ALCOHOL ABUSE

Al-Anon Family Headquarters
1600 Corporate Landing Parkway
Virginia Beach, VA 23454-5617
(800) 4AL-ANON

Alcoholics Anonymous (AA)
General Service Office
475 Riverside Dr.
New York, NY 10115
(212) 870-3400

Children of Alcoholics Foundation
33 West 60th St., 5th Floor
New York, NY 10023
(212) 757-2100 ext. 6370
(212) 757-2208 (fax)
(800) 359-COAF

Meridian Council, Inc.
Administrative Offices
4 Elmcrest Terrace
Norwalk, CT 06850

Mothers Against Drunk Driving (MADD)
(254) 690-6233

National Association of Children of Alcoholics (NACOA)
11426 Rockville Pike, Ste. 100
Rockville, MD 20852
(301) 468-0985
(888) 554-2627

National Clearinghouse for Alcohol and Drug Information (NCADI)
P.O. Box 234
Rockville, MD 20852
(301) 468-2600

National Council on Alcoholism and Drug Dependency (NCADD)
12 West 21st St.
New York, NY 10010
(212) 206-6770

National Council on Alcohol & Drugs
(800) 475-HOPE

Women for Sobriety
(800) 333-1606

ANOREXIA/BULIMIA

American Anorexia/Bulimia Association, Inc.
293 Central Park West, Ste. 1R
New York, NY 10024
(212) 575-6200

Eating Disorder Organization
6655 S. Yale Ave.
Tulsa, OK 74136
(918) 481-4044

CANCER

National Cancer Institute
(800) 4-CANCER

CHILDREN'S ISSUES

Child Molestation

Adults Molested As Children United (AMACU)
232 East Gish Rd.
San Jose, CA 95112
(800) 422-4453

National Committee for Prevention of Child Abuse
332 South Michigan Ave., Ste. 1600
Chicago, IL 60604
(312) 663-3520

Children's and Teens' Crisis Intervention

Boy's Town Crisis Hotline
(800) 448-3000

Children of the Night
(800) 551-1300

Covenant House Hotline
(800) 999-9999

Kid Save
(800) 543-7283

National Runaway and Suicide Hotline
(800) 448-3000

Youth Nineline
(Referrals for parents/teens about drugs, homelessness, runaways)
(800) 999-9999

~ ~ ~

Missing Children

Missing Children-Help Center
410 Ware Blvd., Ste. 400
Tampa, FL 33619
(800) USA-KIDS

National Center for Missing and Exploited Children
1835 K St. NW
Washington, DC 20006
(800) 843-5678

~ ~ ~

Children with Serious Illnesses (fulfilling wishes)

Brass Ring Society
National Headquarters
551 East Semoran Blvd., Ste. E-5
Fern Park, FL 32730
(407) 339-6188
(800) 666-WISH

Make-a-Wish Foundation
(800) 332-9474

~ ~ ~

CO-DEPENDENCY

Co-Dependents Anonymous
(602) 277-7991

~ ~ ~

DEATH/GRIEVING/ SUICIDE

Grief Recovery Helpline
(800) 445-4808

Grief Recovery Institute
8306 Wilshire Blvd., Ste. 21A
Beverly Hills, CA 90211
(213) 650-1234

National Hospice Organization (NHO)
1901 Moore St. #901
Arlington, VA 22209
(703) 243-5900

National Sudden Infant Death Syndrome
Two Metro Plaza, Ste. 205
Landover, MD 20785
(800) 221-SIDS

Seasons: Suicide Bereavement
P.O. Box 187
Park City, UT 84060
(801) 649-8327

Share
(Recovering from violent death of friend or family member)
100 E 8th St., Ste. B41
Cincinnati, OH 45202
(513) 721-5683

Survivors of Suicide
Call your local Mental Health Association for the branch nearest you.

Widowed Persons Service
(202) 434-2260
(800) 424-3410 ext. 2260

DEBTS

Credit Referral
(Information on local credit counseling services)
(800) 388-CCCS

Debtors Anonymous
General Service Office
P.O. Box 400
Grand Central Station
New York, NY 10163-0400
(212) 642-8220

DIABETES

American Diabetes Association
(800) 232-3472

∽ ∽ ∽

DOMESTIC VIOLENCE

National Coalition Against Domestic Violence
P.O. Box 34103
Washington, DC 20043-4103
(202) 544-7358

National Domestic Violence Hotline
(800) 799-SAFE

∽ ∽ ∽

DRUG ABUSE

Cocaine Anonymous
(800) 347-8998

National Cocaine-Abuse Hotline
(800) 262-2463
(800) COCAINE

National Institute of Drug Abuse (NIDA)
Parklawn Building
5600 Fishers Lane,
Room 10A-39
Rockville, MD 20852
(301) 443-6245
(for information)
(800) 662-4357 (for help)

World Service Office (CA)
3740 Overland Ave., Ste. C
Los Angeles, CA 90034-6337
(310) 559-5833
(800) 347-8998
(to leave message)

∽ ∽ ∽

EATING DISORDERS

Eating Disorder Organization
6655 S. Yale Ave.
Tulsa, OK 74136
(918) 481-4044

Overeaters Anonymous
National Office
P.O. Box 44020
Rio Rancho, NM 87174-4020
(505) 891-2664

∽ ∽ ∽

GAMBLING

Gamblers Anonymous
National Council on Compulsive Gambling
444 West 59th St., Room 1521
New York, NY 10019
(212) 903-4400

HEALTH ISSUES

Alzheimer's Disease Information
(800) 621-0379

American Chronic Pain Association
P.O. Box 850
Rocklin, CA 95677
(916) 632-0922

American Foundation of Traditional Chinese Medicine
505 Beach St.
San Francisco, CA 94133
(415) 776-0502

American Holistic Health Association
P.O. Box 17400
Anaheim, CA 92817
(714) 779-6152

Chopra Center for Well Being
Deepak Chopra, M.D.
7630 Fay Ave.
La Jolla, CA 92037
(619) 551-7788

The Fetzer Institute
9292 West KL Ave.
Kalamazoo, MI 49009
(616) 375-2000

Hippocrates Health Institute
1443 Palmdale Court
West Palm Beach, FL 33411
(561) 471-8876

Hospicelink
(800) 331-1620

Institute for Noetic Sciences
P.O. Box 909, Dept. M
Sausalito, CA 94966-0909
(800) 383-1394

The Mind-Body Medical Institute
185 Pilgrim Rd.
Boston, MA 02215
(617) 632-9525

National Health Information Center
P.O. Box 1133
Washington, DC 20013-1133
(800) 336-4797

Optimum Health Care Institute
6970 Central Ave.
Lemon Grove, CA 91945
(619) 464-3346

Preventive Medicine Research Institute
Dean Ornish, M.D.
900 Bridgeway, Ste. 2
Sausalito, CA 94965
(415) 332-2525

World Research Foundation
20501 Ventura Blvd., Ste. 100
Woodland Hills, CA 91364
(818) 999-5483

HOUSING RESOURCES

Acorn
(Nonprofit network of low- and moderate-income housing)
739 8th St., S.E.
Washington, DC 20003
(202) 547-9292

IMPOTENCE

Impotence Institute of America
P.O. Box 410
Bowie, MD 20718-0410
(800) 669-1603
www.impotenceworld.org

INCEST

Incest Survivors Resource Network International, Inc.
P.O. Box 7375
Las Cruces, NM 88006-7375
(505) 521-4260
(Hours: Monday – Saturday, 2 – 4 P.M. and 11 P.M. – Midnight / Eastern time)

PET BEREAVEMENT

Bide-A-Wee Foundation
410 E. 38th St.
New York, NY 10016
(212) 532-6395

The Animal Medical Center
510 E. 62nd St.
New York, NY 10021
(212) 838-8100

Holistic Animal Consulting Center
29 Lyman Ave.
Staten Island, NY 10305
(718) 720-5548

RAPE/SEXUAL ISSUES

Austin Rape Crisis Center
1824 East Oltorf
Austin, TX 78741
(512) 440-7273

National Council on Sexual Addictions and Compulsivity
1090 S. Northchase Parkway, Ste. 200
South Marietta, GA 30067
(770) 989-9754

Sexually Transmitted Disease Referral
(800) 227-8922

SMOKING

Nicotine Anonymous
2118 Greenwich St.
San Francisco, CA 94123
(415) 750-0328

STRESS REDUCTION

The Biofeedback & Psychophysiology Clinic
The Menninger Clinic
P.O. Box 829
Topeka, KS 66601-0829
(913) 350-5000

New York Open Center
(In-depth workshops to invigorate the spirit)
83 Spring St.
New York, NY 10012
(212) 219-2527

Omega Institute
(A healing, spiritual retreat community)
260 Lake Dr.
Rhinebeck, NY 12572-3212
(914) 266-4444 (info)
(800) 944-1001 (to enroll)

Rise Institute
P.O. Box 2733
Petaluma, CA 94973
(707) 765-2758

The Stress Reduction Clinic
Center for Mindfulness
University of Massachusetts Medical Center
55 Lake Ave. North
Worcester, MA 01655
(508) 856-1616
(508) 856-2656

About the Author

Dianne Schwartz, the survivor of an abusive marriage, is the founder and president of Educating Against Domestic Violence, Inc. (EADV), a nonprofit organization providing assistance to battered persons. She is available for presentations on the subject to organizations and educational institutions, and can be reached through her Website at **www.eadv.net** or through the Hay House publicity department.

Dianne lives with her husband, David, in Ohio.

We hope you enjoyed this Hay House book.
If you would like to receive a free catalog featuring additional Hay House books and products, or if you would like information about the Hay Foundation, please contact:

Hay House, Inc.
P.O. Box 5100
Carlsbad, CA 92018-5100

(760) 431-7695 or **(800) 654-5126**
(760) 431-6948 (fax) or **(800) 650-5115 (fax)**

Please visit the Hay House Website at:
www.hayhouse.com